JOHN DUNS SCOTUS
MARY'S ARCHITECT

VENERABLE JOHN DUNS SCOTUS

JOHN DUNS SCOTUS
MARY'S ARCHITECT

by

Allan B. Wolter, O.F.M.

and

Blane O'Neill, O.F.M.

Franciscan Press

Quincy University
1800 College Avenue
Quincy, Illinois 62301-2699

Library of Congress Cataloging-in-Publication Data

Wolter, Allan Bernard, 1913-
    John Duns Scotus : Mary's Architect / by Allan B. Wolter
and Blane O'Neill.
        p.   cm.
    1. Duns Scotus, John, ca. 1266-1308. 2. Individualism.
I. O'Neill, Blane, 1924-   .   II. Title.
B765.D74W57   1993
189'. 4—dc20   92—44732
                                                  CIP

ISBN   0-8199-0960-2

Cover painting by Michael Balkenbush, O.F.M.
Cover photo by Antonine Correa, O.F.M.
Cover design by Thomas More Brown, O.F.M.

This work is dedicated to
our sister and brother Franciscans the world over.

CONTENTS

FOREWORD

At the outset of this work it was the intention of the authors to bring to a more popular audience the work of Fr. Allan Wolter on one of the greatest philosophers of the Middle Ages, namely, John Duns Scotus. Exactly what might be the interest of this medieval philosopher-theologian to a modern audience in the United States was a problem eventually faced by taking a subject of current interest to ascertain how Scotus' work might be applied to it, thereby revealing both the modern problem and Scotus' solution.

The subject chosen was that of individualism as it reveals itself in the history of the United States. Amid the hue and the cry against the individualism rampant today and the call for emphasis on community, it seemed most fruitful to learn what the recently proclaimed "Blessed" Scotsman might have to offer both this time and this place.

In keeping with the popularization, we have opted to drop the critical apparatus of footnoting, inserting immediately into the text whatever reference is necessary.

Admittedly, the text at times does plumb the depths. Such abstraction and in-depth writing is occasioned by the consideration that Scotus is, after all, the "Subtle Doctor." If he is to be done justice, there should be a sampling of what his sublety truly is.

It is the hope of the authors that there will emerge a clear picture of this medieval genius, of the work he accomplished during his short forty-two years on this earth, and how he can offer, especially to Franciscans, a guideline for the facing of an American problem.

A special debt of gratitude is owed to Mrs. Bea Schwab who so faithfully read, counseled, and encouraged this work. A debt is owed likewise to the Franciscan community of Old Mission Santa Barbara, especially to Fathers Tom Messner, Bill Haney, and Alberic Smith. Not the least of those who have encourage this work have been the Franciscans Father Ladislaus Siekaniec of Sacred Heart Province and Father Alan McCoy of St. Barbara Province.

INTRODUCTION

Mention the name John Duns Scotus these days and the responses are interesting, or at least varied. "John Duns who?" asks a Catholic layman, having heard the name for the first time. A priest, busy with parochial matters, upon hearing the name Scotus, pauses for a moment, crinkles his face, and comments that he just vaguely recalls the name from the philosophy course that was part of the curriculum during his seminary training.

"What more can be said about Scotus?" asks the historian of medieval philosophy or theology, well aware that university libraries are replete with tomes of his works and lore about his person. Much has been written of his thought, both pro and con. Dubbed by his colleagues as "Subtle Doctor" because of acuteness of mind, John is known as the "Marian Doctor" because of his role in the declaration of the Immaculate Conception of the Blessed Virgin Mary as a dogma of the Roman Catholic Church. There are those, like the American scientist-philosopher C. S. Peirce, who consider Duns Scotus the greatest metaphysician of all times. Others in the past have disagreed. But referring to such, that eminent member of the French Academy, the late Etienne Gilson, declared: "Of a hundred writers who have held Duns Scotus up to ridicule, not two of them have ever read him, and not one of them has understood him."

Were one to travel to the unassuming Scottish town of Duns in the district called Berwick, close to the North Sea in the borderlands between Scotland and England, he would discover the ancestral home of John Duns, the Scotsman (for *Scotus* is Latin for "the Scot"). In the official guidebook of the town of Duns, there is the not insignificant entry:

> Also near the entrance to the Park [public park] is a fine bronze statue of the most famous native of the town, John Duns Scotus, the great medieval philosopher and theologian. This statue was gifted to the town by the members of the Franciscan Order in 1966 to commemorate the seven hundredth anniversary of the birth of the great scholar.

No fewer than twelve supreme pontiffs of the Roman Catholic Church, from Alexander VI in 1501 to John Paul II in 1980, have endorsed the teachings of Scotus as one of the glories of the Franciscan Order. Pope Paul VI, on the occasion of the 700th anniversary of Scotus' birth, voiced

1

his deep conviction that "the valuable theological treasure of John Duns Scotus can provide formidable weapons in the struggle to disperse the black cloud of atheism which hangs darkly over our age." The Holy Father also expresses the hope that the "teachings of Scotus may perhaps provide a golden framework for serious dialogue between the Catholic Church and the Anglican Communion as well as other Christian communities of Great Britain."

Most recently there has appeared in the London *Tablet* (February 9, 91) a notice that the Scottish clergy, realizing what a glory Scotus is to Scotland, are concerned with his canonization and are setting out to do something to make that canonization a reality. And Pope John Paul II has facilitated their efforts by officially recognizing John Duns as "blessed" by reason of his cult "from time immemorial," the equivalent of a formal process of beatification. Only a proven miracle through his intercession is now required for official canonization.

Twenty-five years have elapsed since the *Alma Parens* of Pope Paul VI expressed such exalted hopes for the influence of Scotus. Perhaps those desires will be realized more than might be expected, not only in Scotland and the rest of the British Isles, but also on this side of the Atlantic where over the last two centuries there has been a sharing of the heritage of which Scotus is so much a part.

The purpose of this present work is to accomplish two things: first, to explore a problem that currently deeply disturbs many concerned citizens in the United States. Secondly, by an examination of the life and significant works of Blessed John Duns Scotus we hope to find insightful guidelines that may help to solve this problem, especially for those of us who, like Bl. John, profess to be followers of the Poverello, St. Francis of Assisi. For as Pope Paul VI reminds us: "Following in the wake of more than fifty Franciscan scholastics, [Scotus] assimilated and perfected their teachings and excelled them all, becoming the principal standard-bearer of the Franciscan School." For the pope envisioned Scotus as another architect constructing a theological temple, like Aquinas a generation before him. If we lament the fact that Duns' early death left most of his major writings incomplete, we are grateful, at least, for "the valuable theological treasure" in the two major works that have come down to us, since these contain the architectural blueprints for building a better world in our own day.

Part I

THE CURRENT SCENE

POPULAR COMPLAINTS

In the United States these days there is a variously-expressed but recurring lament: We need a balance between "individualism" and "community." For instance, *Time* magazine (February 25, 91) presents the case of Amitai Etzioni at George Washington University who is exasperated with what he sees as the "selfish individualism" he finds in groups such as the A.C.L.U. libertarians and other radical individualists. Etzioni calls for the establishment of a group that will uphold "community" to offset the exaggerated emphasis on the "rights of the individual." The February 91 issue of *Harpers* features a roundtable discussion among four professors, a mayor, and an editor at Independence Hall in Philadelphia during the bicentennial year of the passage of the Bill of Rights. The purpose of their gathering within these hallowed walls was to speculate on whether there is a need for a "Bill of Duties" as well as a Bill of Rights for the country.

Day after day, the nation witnesses media reports about people demanding, even suing to obtain, their rights. Doctors are forced to take out malpractice insurance in the likelihood that they will be sued. For some, the vilest word in the language is "censorship" of my right to say what I want.

William F. Buckley, Jr.'s new book, *Gratitude: Reflections On What We Owe Our Country*, focuses on the trend toward the self indulgent pursuit of pleasure as a way of life (hedonism) in the United States. The younger generation, without a sense of gratitude for what they have received, will soon be the adults of the country. Buckley is anxious to aid in the development of a moral society which would be characterized by its willingness to help others. To that end he suggests how the youth of America might be directed to use its talents in the service of the country.

The Los Angeles *Times* (October 16, 90) in an article entitled "Young America is Looking Out for No. 1" featured a report from the Josephson Institute of Ethics. According to the eighty-page report, there is a sad lack of ethics in the current generation of eighteen-thirty-year olds. The "IDIs" (I Deserve Its) "act as if they need whatever they want and deserve whatever they need, as if winning is a basic right." Saddest about the report is the fact that although Josephson was anticipating violent reactions both to the Report and to his TV interviews concerning it, he was swamped with calls that he had not gone far enough.

In early May of 1991, a work bearing the title *The Day America Told The Truth*, by James Patterson and Peter Kim, began to appear in bookstores around the U.S. It is a volume that purports to be the largest survey of the private morals of Americans ever undertaken. Including topics such as drugs, family life, secrets, crime, marriage, the death penalty, lying, patriotism, suicide, the work ethic, and our sense of community, the survey asked its respondents questions about matters such as private sexual fantasies, what people will do for ten million dollars, and the secrets we keep from our families. The picture that emerges fits well with what social critics have come to identify as a situation in which there is a breakdown in the former balance between the rights and duties of the individual and those of society. At present in the United States there is great concern in popular literature with the overstressing of the individual.

HABITS OF THE HEART

In the light of the problem outlined above, there have been studies which look not only to the symptoms of a problem but also to its roots. What might be called the bible concerning the problem presented by exaggerated individualism is Robert Bellah and associates' 1985 work *Habits of the Heart: Individualism and Commitment in American Life*. The work seeks in-depth interviewing of people from all parts of the country to ascertain where we stand currently. Having discovered the strong "individualistic" spirit of the nation, and its consequent dangers, the authors set about tracing this spirit historically, beginning with the classic criticism of our new nation by the perceptive French author and statesman, Alexis de Tocqueville (1805-59). Already in the last century, Tocqueville had noticed a possible flaw in the country's makeup, namely, the tendency of the citizens to leave the marketplace and return to the privacy of the family; the rest of society could take care of itself. Such an individualistic tendency could prove dangerous. De Tocqueville, however, is not referring to egotism which is simply selfishness, dating roughly to the time of Adam and Eve. Rather, the "individualism" of which he speaks consists in an erroneous judgment of democratic origin.

In the early days of the nation the strong presence of the churches here and there and everywhere, as well as the republican notion of the "common good," were powerful enough influences to defuse the dangers of individualistic self serving.

By 1840, there developed what Bellah refers to as two forms of individualism. The first is called "utilitarian," as exemplified in the life of Ben

Franklin (poor boy makes good). If each person vigorously pursues his own good, uses his talents industriously as did Poor Richard of *Almanac* fame, there automatically emerges the social good.

A second form of individualism is called "expressive." This is the type championed by Emerson, Thoreau, and Whitman who on the one hand feared that Franklin's outlook was too materialistic and on the other that social institutions would warp the individual's self expression. Ralph Waldo Emerson preached "Self-Reliance"; Henry David Thoreau retreated to the solitary (?) confines of Walden Pond; Walt Whitman in his self-printed *Leaves of Grass* sang the varied carols of America, especially in the "Song of Myself."

In the crucible of history, couple the above two forms of individualism; mix in a generous portion of western expansion and rugged individualism; add the acrid commercialism of the Industrial Revolution which has succeeded in breaking down the former influence of religion; let ferment for a few decades—the result is guaranteed to fragment the entire society. Or, as Bellah reminds us, examine our traditions of "life," "liberty," and the "pursuit of happiness." *Habits of the Heart* finds that "life" is the "good life," in the sense of economic progress, to be procured in any way possible. "Liberty," our most cherished value, has come to mean "being left alone while we are doing our own thing." "The pursuit of happiness" is understood in the sense that every individual has the opportunity to pursue whatever he or she considers happiness. In the midst of everyone's doing his or her own thing, what is needed is a vision.

BEYOND INDIVIDUALISM

Previously we have referred to *The Day America Told the Truth* as a survey of private morals. More specifically, from the viewpoint of morality, Patterson and Kim report,

> "We [Americans] have established ourselves as the authority on morality. We now choose which commandments to believe and which ones not to believe. Clearly, the God of the 1990s in America is a distant and pale reflection of the God of our forefathers. This is not the "Jealous God" of the Old Testament—six in seven people think that it is okay not to believe in God. Rather, Americans seem to use God to refer to a general principle of good in life—or sometimes He (or She) is the creator who set off the Big Bang but doesn't intervene in human affairs.
>
> For most Americans, God is not to be feared or, for that matter, loved." (p.201)

There are several ways in which contemporary Catholic thinkers have attempted to find a strategy that can serve to correct the imbalance between the individual and society that obtains in this nation today, by going back to an earlier age for a set of values we have lost sight of.

One recent attempt is found in the work entitled *Beyond Individualism: A Retrieval of Moral Discourse in America*, edited by Donald L. Gelpi, S.J. He sees the problem as primarily American and looks to an earlier specifically American philosopher and theologian, Jonathan Edwards, for inspiration. He finds it in Edwards' concern with "conversion" which he expands with insights from modern theology. Jonathan's personal conversion was his rejection of the Calvinistic pessimistic conception of predetermination, and acceptance of personal responsibility to live for God and others instead of just for oneself. His ministry was helping converts to do the same, convinced, as he was, that by the working of the Holy Spirit they will come to see and love the beauty of God in the Lord Jesus incarnate and in the lives of those who resemble Jesus. Gelpi and his co-authors show how this religious "conversion" can be expanded to include all areas of responsibility that are revealed to us by modern theology and that strike at the heart of privatized religion. For example, affective (personal responsibility for the health of one's emotions), intellectual (responsibility for the truth or falsity of personal judgments), moral (responsibility for responding to God in faith), and sociopolitical (responsibility for influencing the decisions of others, e.g., getting large corporations to help in the eliminating of world hunger, of working for world peace, of upholding the rights of minorities).

In contrast to this specifically American approach is that of Ewert Cousins, who sees the problem in its global aspects. Before the first millennium B.C., mankind was community oriented, with little or no awareness of personal identity or any sharply defined notion of the individual self. The consciousness of archaic peoples was closely knit to the whole of nature. Individuals were integral members of a family, which was itself but a portion of the tribe, and the tribe itself felt its close kinship with the animal kingdom, the inorganic world, and the cosmos. But, as the existentialist philosopher Karl Jaspers in his study *The Origin and Goal of History* pointed out, somewhere between 800 B.C. and 200 B.C. an amazing transformation of human consciousness took place in which man became conscious of his individuality and self identity. This spiritual transformation, he notes, originated independently in three geographical areas (China, central Asia, and the eastern Mediterranean). Jaspers locates the temporal axis of this historical transformation around 500 B.C. "It is there we meet with the most deepcut dividing line in history. Man, as we know him today, came into being. For short, we may style this the 'Axial Period.'" During the age that followed, as Jaspers notes, "were born the fundamental categories within which we still think today, and the beginnings of the world religions, by which human beings still live, were created.'' In the twenty centuries that followed this awakening of mankind's sense of individuality, its recognition of personal independence, rational creativity, and moral responsibility brought many blessings to the civilized world. But it also created problems, alienating the human person from the cosmos and community.

Today, on the eve of the twenty-first century, a new transformation of consciousness is needed. For we have entered the space age and can see from the eyes of the astronaut that our earth is mankind's God-given space ship for its journey through history. No longer can we tolerate the exploitation of its limited life sustaining resources by egotistic individuals, by local groups, by rival sovereignties, or multinational organizations. We live in an interdependent world in which rugged individualism in any shape or form has no future. Cousins, then, sees us entering that second Axial Period, the transition from individual to global consciousness, that will bring back an awareness of community and the recognition that our earth and its resources are the common property of the human race.

As a spiritual affiliate of Holy Name Province of the Order of Friars Minor, Cousins sees the world on the eve of the twenty-first century through the eyes of St. Francis for whom every item in the world was either a brother or sister. Ewert views Franciscan philosophy as playing a vital ecumenical role that he hopes to promote as the general editor of an ongoing twenty-five volume series of studies entitled, *World Spirituality: An Encyclopedic History of the Religious Quest*. A specialist in the thought of St. Bonaventure, he has understandably shown the openness of his Christocentric theology to a meeting with Eastern spiritual mysticism.

Other Franciscan thinkers held similar views of the earth as the common property of the human race, and the need to balance our unique value as individuals with our social obligations. John Duns Scotus was one such philosophical theologian whose Christocentrism went even farther than that of Bonaventure.

In this present work, we wish to present a game-plan based on the philosophical theology of John Duns Scotus that provides an even more cogent traditional basis for solving our national problem than Gelpi's Edwardian adaptation or Cousins' broader Bonaventurian-based Franciscan solution. For, as Pope Paul VI notes in his Apostolic Letter *Alma Parens*: ''It is universally recognized that John Duns Scotus surpassed the Seraphic Doctor.''

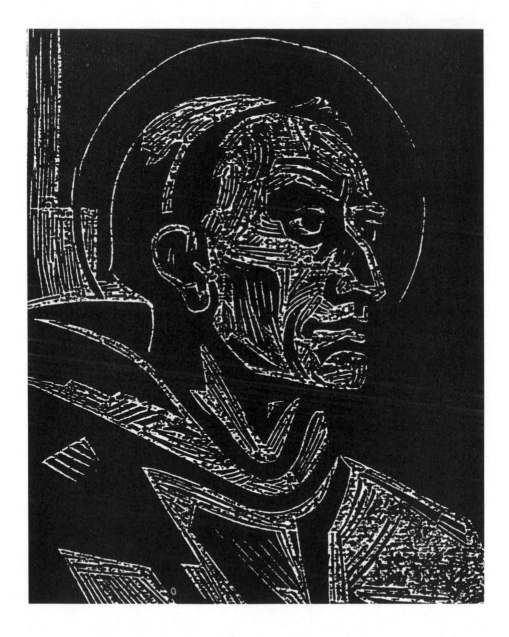

Part II

THE ARCHITECT

In his apostolic letter *Alma Parens (Devoted Mother)*, written on the occasion of Scotus' seventh centenary celebration in Oxford, England, and in Duns, and Edinburgh, Scotland, Pope Paul VI compared him to St. Thomas Aquinas, likening the works of each to a temple:

> Beside the principal and magnificent temple, which is of St. Thomas Aquinas, there are others, among which, although differing from it in style and size, is that splendid temple which John Duns Scotus, with his ardent and contemplative genius, based on solid foundations and built up with daring pinnacles pointing towards heaven.

As the Holy Father sees him, Scotus is an architect, responsible for a structure solidly based on firm foundations, supporting a superstructure whose lines direct the eye heavenward. Such a description calls to mind a picture of the medieval Gothic temples that once dominated the skylines of city and town in the Western world. Today, buildings such as these in metropolitan centers, especially in the United States, have long since been overshadowed by the towers of commerce. Steeples triangular in outline that silently shouted the presence of the Holy Trinity have long since been shaded by the gleaming glass and steel spires of the world of business.

From the viewpoint of the civilization that has developed in our day, we think it most fitting, for Americans in general but particularly for those who, like Bl. John Duns, profess to be followers of the Poverello of Assisi, to pause to consider what philosophical and theological insights he can provide for correcting the imbalance between what we owe to self and what we owe to society. Lest our reconstruction be just another house built on sand, let us examine his own life and works for building clues, for the philosophical and theological foundation stones we need. Unlike Aquinas and other theologians, he did not regard theology as a theoretic or speculative discipline, but rather as a practical guide based on a sound metaphysical conception of what God is and the Franciscan faith-vision of what we are, created in the image and likeness of the Trinity, destined to share someday in their inner personal life through our kinship with Christ, the first born of God's cosmic creation. In the architectural model with its "daring pinnacles" that he constructs for us, we see spelled out a comprehensive plan of life that will lead not only to our own self fulfillment, but socially to "new heavens and a new earth" (Revelation, 22:1).

Early Life

It is a paradox that as we approach the life of one who in ages past has climbed the heights of his own era, we are met with the biographer's lament, "Not much is known of the life of..." True, in our age of "gleaming glass and steel spires" we keep better records than did they of seven centuries past. But even we, like them, have learned that since it takes a while for most people to make their mark on history, even we do not think to record until someone is called to our attention. Often, by then it is too late to ascertain the interesting details that would have proved so informative.

The popular Latin summary of the life of John Duns Scotus engraved on his tomb reads: "*Scotia me genuit.*" [Scotland begot me.] "*Anglia me suscepit.*" [England reared me.] "*Gallia me docuit.*" [France taught me.] "*Colonia me tenet.*" [Cologne holds my remains.] And such is the overall picture. To be sure, there have been those who have claimed that Scotus was from England or from Ireland; but recent scholarship names Scotland. For when Scotus was living in the Franciscan friary at the University of Paris, there were no fewer than forty other friars by the name of John. To distinguish him, he was called by the name "Scotus" which means a native of Scotland, the land of Robert Bruce, of the Earl of Douglas, of Bobby Burns and of Sir Walter Scott.

Not surprisingly, among those who regarded this defender of Mary's sinlessness as a saint, pious legends grew. Some portray him as a simple shepherd lad, blessed with visions of the Blessed Mother in childhood. These led him one day to argue so persuasively as to set in motion a devotion of the faithful that would eventually bring about the declaration of her Immaculate Conception. Current studies are more critical in defending such claims, and stress rather the limited but more certain information that can be gleaned from probing the hundreds of medieval manuscripts of his writings still preserved in libraries throughout the Western world. Historians are now agreed that he was of the family of Duns and was born in a little town of the same name, nestled between the Lammermuir and Cheviot Hills, close to the North Sea and the Scottish-English border in the district of Berwick. The Tweed River runs nearby. At the end of Castle Street, to the northwest of the city, there lies Duns Castle, next to the old town of Duns. Near the castle is an historical marker indicating the site of Bl. John's birthplace in the year 1266, three years after King Alexander and his Scotsmen had driven off the Danish pirates.

It may well be that young John, clad in a kilt of tartan wool in the colors of his clan and sporting a tam o'shanter, could have been heard saying something like: "Laird, heir I cum!" as he visited one of the nearby abbeys. Like sentinels standing guard, not far from Duns were Melrose Abbey (St. Mary's), occupied by the Cistercians; Dryburgh Abbey of the Premonstratensians; Kelso of the Benedictines; and Jedburgh of the Canons Regular of St. Augustine. Scotus' later comment in his famed *Opus Oxoniense* concerning things pertaining to worship gives us to believe that he was involved in the nearby abbeys.

> In the primitive Church the children were not introduced at an early age to the matters surrounding cult and the divine liturgy. Moreover, adults were all too ignorant of these matters. Today, on the contrary, children are soon introduced to cult and are practiced in it. Thus it is at the present time those who are thirteen years of age are better instructed in sacred matters than perhaps an adult twenty years old was then.

Of Scotus' early life, historian John Major states that "when he was no more than a boy, but had already been grounded in grammar, he was taken by two Scottish Minorite [Franciscan] friars to Oxford." There he was received into the convent as a *puer oblatus* (postulant), continuing his studies under the friars until he was old enough to enter the Order. Young Duns may well have had some close relative among the Franciscans who early recognized his exceptional intellectual talents, perhaps one of the friars who brought him to Oxford. How else would he have been attracted to their form of religious life or been able to pierce the line of the Cistercians, Premonstratensians, Benedictines, and Canons Regular of St. Augustine that stood guard between Duns and his future home in England. Whatever the case, John Duns came early to that university city where he was steeped in the principles that would qualify him as one of the world's great architects.

Oxford

"Towery city and branchy between towers" are the words with which the great British poet, Jesuit Gerard Manley Hopkins, describes the skyline of Oxford in his sonnet *Duns Scotus's Oxford*. Tree branches fill the spaces between the spires. To Hopkins, however, the most important thing about Oxford is neither its architecture nor the sounds of the city but rather the fact that Scotus had been there:

> Yet ah! this air I gather and release
> He lived on; these weeds and waters, these walls are what
> He haunted who of all men sways my spirit to peace.

Hopkins had pored over the blueprints of Scotus' temple and discovered a kindred spirit. The building block of *individuation*, so native to Scotus, was the same which Hopkins identified with the *inscape* and *instress* distinctive of his own poetic edifice. Of Scotus' insight into things Hopkins is convinced that there has never been an insight to rival it,

"be rival Italy [Aquinas] or Greece" [Aristotle].

Boys as young as twelve could begin their studies at Oxford. Scotus' earlier remark about a thirteen-year old's knowledge of sacred matters may be indicative of his own experience. If the Oxford friary was the source of his familiarity with such, he may well have begun his undergraduate studies in philosophy and the liberal arts as early as 1278. Having come to Oxford in 1224, the Franciscans had long since become firmly ensconced at that university and involved in the educational apostolate. They had been welcomed there by its first recorded chancellor, Robert Grosseteste, the remarkable, intellectually original theologian largely responsible for the mathematical-scientific orientation of the university and the introduction of Aristotle's works on the natural sciences to its official syllabus, when these were still prohibited to be read at Paris. Friend of all the newfounded mendicant orders, he was a special benefactor to the Franciscans who regarded him as the founder of their Oxford school. For at the request of Friar Adam Marsh, his student, he gave them special lectures in theology and later, as bishop of Lincoln, bequeathed to their friary his valuable library.

State of the Franciscan Order in England

How the Franciscans (known as the Greyfriars because of the color of their habit) came to England and by the time of Scotus were so prominently involved in university life at Oxford and Cambridge is an interesting chapter in the history of their Order. It was on Tuesday, September 10, 1224, that the first nine friars landed in Dover from France and headed directly for Canterbury, the see city of England. Departing immediately for London and Oxford, they thought that these would be the likely places in which to most easily attract recruits. In these cities, living lives of strict poverty and simplicity, the friars at times walked miles barefooted through the snow, leaving blood-stained trails. Sans shoes, money, and houses, yet remarkably cheerful, the friars of the early days in England witnessed to the life of St. Francis of Assisi, passing on the tradition to those who came in such droves after them.

Between 1225 and 1230, the Greyfriars branched out to Norwich, Worcester, Hereford, Salisbury, York, Lincoln, Bristol, Lynn, Gloucester, Nottingham, Leicester, and Stamford and shortly thereafter to Chichester, Carlisle, Winchester, Lichfield, and Exeter. Living in ordinary houses or make-shift huts, they worked among the sick and the poor; they were sincere and austere. Says historian A. G. Little, "Certainly at first the friars in England revelled in poverty with a zeal which may well have cheered the heart of St. Francis in his last sad days."

Much of the outstanding example of the followers of Francis in the early days in England was owing to their first leaders: Agnellus of Pisa (who brought them to England); Albert of Pisa, Haymo of Faversham, and William of Nottingham. Between 1224 and 1254 there were eight custodies (or territorial divisions of friaries) which together made up the English province, including six friaries in Scotland. According to historian Thomas Eccleston, by 1255 there were 1242 friars in England and Scotland. It was of this English province that the minister general, John of Parma, after his visitation of the province in 1250, said: "How I wish that a province such as this could be set in the center of the world and provide an example to the whole Order."

As said before, the friars came to Oxford because they thought that at the university they would be able to attract suitable recruits to the Order. And attract them they did! Nine years after the arrival of the friars in England there were forty friars stationed at the Franciscan friary at Oxford. Surely it wasn't studies that attracted the idealistic young men to the poor and humble friars. Rather, something there was about the Franciscan cheerfulness of community life and profound dedication to the values of the Gospel that drew followers. Even intellectuals in the university community like Robert Grosseteste and his student Adam Marsh were not immune to their appeal. The one felt privileged to teach them, the other would become the first Franciscan master of theology.

Enters Franciscan Order

It was to this Oxford friary that Scotus first came as postulant, attracted to the Franciscan way of life. At eighteen, during his study years of the arts and natural sciences, he would have become old enough to enter the novitiate, probably in the year 1284, and a year later take solemn vows in the Order of Friars Minor.

It is somewhat difficult to see how John Duns, so much unlike Francis in temperament and upbringing, could be attracted to the poor and humble life of the friars. Perhaps it wasn't Francis himself to whom he was attracted but to the friars of his own part of the world. For the most part, these were very sharp young men, drawn to the service of the Church through studies that were taught in a warm, challenging, and seraphic environment. The majority of the friars entered the clerical state in England at the time of Scotus, and the brightest of these went to the universities for teacher training. The friars who brought him to Oxford must have been educated men who recognized his talents and aptitude for higher studies. But if Scotus wasn't drawn to the friars by the example of Francis, at least at Oxford he was exposed to the highest of Franciscan traditions, in *doctrina et sanctitate* (learning and holiness), the ideals of the Poverello and the heights of academia. Somewhere along the line he imbibed the principles on which he would construct his masterpiece. The temple which resulted proclaims at every pillar and pinnacle the glory and honor of God. But if we look closely, we will discover the fingerprints of the little poor man of Assisi.

Theological Studies preceding Ordination

After completing his studies in Aristotle's philosophy and in the natural sciences, he began in October of 1288 the thirteen-year program of theological studies that would lead to a doctoral or master's degree. The first six years were devoted to what we might call the passive study of theology, perhaps somewhat more advanced than a seminarian might receive today in preparation for pastoral ministry among the faithful; the last seven would be more like the graduate studies required today for a professional theologian or a doctorate in theology. The first three years devoted to biblical studies were all that most priests would need to preach and administer the sacraments. Sometime during those years he would have received minor orders and, when old enough canonically, the sub-deaconate and deaconate. When and where we do not know, but one of the happy discoveries of Father Ephrem Longpré O.F.M., is the record of John Duns' ordination to the priesthood.

Scotus' Ordination at Northhampton

Oxford was in the diocese of Lincoln, and records in the episcopal archives indicate that Bishop Oliver Sutton on March 17, 1291, held ordination ceremonies for minor and major Holy Orders in the Benedictine priory church of St. Andrew in Northampton. John Duns was one of the five Franciscan priests ordained on that occasion. This first definite date we have in Bl. John's life, is used to estimate the probable date of his birth. For Bishop Sutton held a similar ordination some months earlier (December 29). Since Scotus was not ordained on that occasion, it is presumed that he had not yet reached the age of twenty-five required by canon law for priestly ordination. This would place his birth most probably in the early months of the year 1266.

It would be interesting to know if the newly ordained theologian was permitted to journey home to Duns for a first Mass celebration with his family in Scotland, or had to return immediately to Oxford as many of those from the university did who received minor orders, the subdeaconate or deaconate from Bishop Sutton on that day in St. Andrew's. If close relatives in the Duns family had come from Berwickshire for the affair, more than likely they would have attended John's first Mass celebrated in the Franciscan friary in Northampton, which housed some forty or more local friars at the time.

Whatever may have been the celebration at the time of his ordination, Bl. John soon returned to the world of studies. He was probably in his third year of biblical studies at the time and the next three years would be devoted to a more systematic study of the whole field of theology based on Peter Lombard's popular collection of patristic opinions or *Sentences*, that had become the standard textbook first at Paris, then at Oxford. Its four books treated a summary of patristic views on the following topics. Book I: God: One and Triune; Book II: Creation, The Fall of the Angels, The Sin of Our First Parents; Book III: Incarnation, Redemption, Virtues, The Ten Commandments; Book IV: Sacraments, The Four Last Things: Death, Judgment, Hell and Heaven, thus giving the theological student a rather comprehensive survey of divergent views of the Fathers of the Church, and suggesting further problems of the traditional theology.

Advanced studies leading to the doctorate.

John would have been around twenty-eight years of age, when he finished his six years of introductory studies of the bible and Lombard's text. At this stage the bachelor began the seven years of more advanced studies, like that of our graduate courses for the doctorate. This would qualify him, if successfully completed, for being licensed as a professional teacher by the chancellor of the university and being received into the guild of masters of theology, the medieval equivalent of a doctoral degree in theology. This began with two years in which the theological candidate played the role of *opponent* and a year that of *respondent* in public disputations supervised by some master. The modern equivalent would be that of a graduate seminar where the students participated in discussing a problem suggested by their professor.

Masters took regular turns conducting these *ordinary disputations* as a means of training their bachelor students and of presenting their own views. For these exercises were a two-day affair. On the first day, the master raised the question and let the bachelors discuss its pros and cons; on the second day he gave his definitive solution or *determinatio*. The formal task of the bachelor opponent on that first day was to raise objections, like a devil's advocate, to the thesis he knew the master would defend, and that of the respondent was to present an initial answer to the arguments of the opponent. If a master had several bachelor aspirants studying under him, there could be a plurality of opponents or respondents involved in the first day's disputation. On the following day, the master would review the previous day's discussion in a more orderly fashion; and after presenting his *determinatio* or definitive solution to the question, he would answer in his own way the arguments that had been raised by the bachelor opponents. Usually each year a master chose a particular topic for the questions he would propose when his turn came. Eventually he would publish a revised edition of these questions he had determined as a single treatise on that subject. These ordinary "disputed questions," as they were called, were distinguished from the more solemn quodlibetal disputation, called a *Quodlibet* where questions discussed could be raised by any participant, be he master, bachelor, or casual auditor, about any theological topic of current interest. Only the most skilled and daring masters engaged in such during their regency, as master Scotus himself would do some day at the University of Paris. But more of that later.

Here we only note that John between his twenty-eighth and thirtieth year crossed swords with other bachelors in stimulating theological debates under the supervision of a regent master, two years as opponent raising objections, and the last in the more difficult role of respondent.

Sententiarius or Lecturer on the *Sentences.*

Thirty years old, a skilled participant in such theological debates, John still needed four more years before his teacher training was complete and he had fulfilled all the necessary preliminaries for being licensed by the chancellor to receive his biretta as a master. John was given the next year (his tenth since beginning his theological studies) to prepare an original set of lectures that would cover the whole field of systematic theology. It was like writing a doctoral dissertation to prove his competence as a teacher. His next year would be spent delivering these as lecturer. The controversial questions he chose to discuss were of current interest. Only because their topical arrangement was made according to the headings and distinctions of the subject matter in the four books of their Lombard textbook, would it be called, somewhat inappropriately, a "Commentary on the *Sentences.*" All four books were commented on in a single school year. The initial lecture on each book was called a *principium.* That on Book I was scheduled for the bachelor's first lecture day in October, the *principium* for each of the remaining three books was scheduled for the beginning lecture day of January, March and May respectively. The subject matter treated in these "commentaries" ranged over the whole field of theology. Hence a theologian's Sentence-commentary, especially if revised and enlarged for publication and distribution to the booksellers as an *Ordinatio*, might be the most comprehensive theological work, topic-wise, that a professional theologian might ever produce. Such, for example, was St. Bonaventure's Commentary on the *Sentences.* The same would be true, almost half a century later, for Duns Scotus or later Franciscan theologians like Peter Auriol or William of Ockham.

It was customary, among the four mendicant orders at least, for the bachelors, chosen as their order's particular *sententiarius* for that year, to give their respective lectures on different days so that they, as well as their auditors, might attend each others' lectures if they desired. At Paris, at least, the first to lecture when the school year began around October 9th was the Carmelite bachelor, followed on the successive class days in turn by the Austin, the Franciscan and the Dominican. Because of this order, these lectures, like the successive disputations of the masters, were called "ordinary"; and the respective bachelor was said to be reading the *Sentences ordinarie* rather than *cursive* as he had done earlier.

In editing these questions discussed in his lectures, it was customary for the bachelor to frame them in that special way that came to be known later as "scholastic." After presenting his question, with an indication of the distinction in Lombard's *Sentences* which had occasioned it, the bachelor modeled his tripartite answer on the two-day ordinary disputation of a master. He began with a short series of arguments against the position he would eventually defend. These initial arguments, called technically *argumenta principalia*, were reminiscent of the arguments proposed by opponents at the beginning of a magisterial disputation. After this list of objections was complete, the bachelor introduced one or more arguments for the opposite view (usually his own), which often began with the phrase "Sed contra" or "Ad oppositum."—This echoes the counterargument(s) of a respondent on the first day of a magisterial disputation.

After this introductory pro and con came the *corpus* or main body of the question, modeled on the second day's determination a master might give. In it the bachelor often reviewed a number of current opinions on the topic, after which he presented his own personal solution to the question, usually introduced by some phrase like "But I say..." that mimicked the definitive solution or *determinatio* of a master. The third and final part, introduced by the Latin phrase *ad argumenta principalia*, was the lecturer's personal solution to the arguments raised against his solution in the introductory pro and con. These too resembled a master's own response to the arguments raised by his bachelor opponents.

Scotus' last years at Oxford.

The requirements, at least at Oxford, stated that after his stint as *sententiarius*, the bachelor was to spend the following year (his twelfth) lecturing on the Bible as *bachalarius biblicus*. In this role he was to familiarize himself further with the text, the biblical commentaries and glosses, in preparation for occupancy of a magisterial chair. For the main task of a regent master would be to lecture, in the early hours (after Prime or six o'clock), on the Scriptures. Masters also had to give occasional sermons to the university community as well as conduct periodically the aforesaid "ordinary disputations" during the academic year. On these occasions the lectures of bachelors were suspended that they might attend either as auditors or more actively as opponents or respondents.

In the final year (the thirteenth) of his training, the fully formed bachelor (*bachalarius formatus*) had to participate in public disputations conducted by different masters besides his own. So much for the preparation required before one could incept as master at Oxford.

It is not clear whether Scotus spent his twelfth year at Oxford as a *bachalarius biblicus*, or whether he was engaged by that time in more practical pursuits such as ministering as a priest to those pilgrims who came to the Franciscan church for spiritual help. For it had become clear by the summer of 1300, two years before John's training was complete, that he would still have a long wait before he could hope to incept as master in Oxford. On the other hand, periodically the English province had the opportunity to send a candidate for the magisterial chair at the more prestigious University of Paris, where every other regent master had to come from a province other than that of France. Since these candidates would have to read the *Sentences* again at Paris, it was customary for the English province to choose a much younger but more talented bachelor in the waiting line for the Paris opening, when it came. John Duns seems to have been just such a choice, for his exceptional talent and brilliance as a teacher was already recognized by both his religious superiors and the academic world as well. We know that Thomas Sutton, regent master of the Dominicans at Oxford, devoted an entire work just to a critique of Book I of Scotus' commentary on the "Sentences."

Scotus' Paris appointment and pastoral ministry.

The Paris appointment had to be made by the minister general himself as head of the Order of Friars Minor. Furthermore, the bachelor selected to read the *Sentences* was usually given a two years' advanced notice in which to prepare his classes. Since John began lecturing on the *Sentences* at Paris in the fall of 1302, he must have been informed of his Paris appointment shortly after finishing his lectures in June 1300.

We know that in the summer of that year he had already begun reworking the material contained in this *Lectura* for publication and general distribution. This greatly enlarged revision, which he dictated to secretaries, is known as his Oxford work (*Opus Oxoniense*), or in the Vatican edition, in contrast to the *Lectura*, as his *Ordinatio*. In the second question of its prologue, which has no parallel in the earlier work and is apparently based on a sermon he had given during the summer months, Scotus explicitly cites 1300 as the year in which he is composing it.

Two events occurred in Oxford around the beginning of summer of that year which indicate John was not only interested in academic pursuits, but also in practical priestly ministry to the faithful who flocked in such great numbers to the friars' church, both to hear their preaching and to receive the sacrament of penance. Since many penitents were pilgrims who had come from afar, and if their sin was of such a more serious nature as to be reserved to the bishop of the diocese, special faculties might be required for confessors to absolve them. It was customary for the bishop to license certain priests for such cases. And this seems to have been the reason that on July 23, 1300, the English provincial himself, Hugh of Hartlepool, met with John Dalderby, bishop of Lincoln, at Dorchester-on-the-Thames. He submitted a list of twenty-two friars, the name of John Duns among them, for receiving such faculties. Amazed as the bishop was at the request for such an unprecedented number of confessors, his first response was to ask the provincial whether this was for all the churches in his diocese, the largest in England. Astounded to hear they were intended solely for the Franciscan church in Oxford, he pointed out to Hugh the unreasonableness of this request. No church in the diocese had ever been given more than three confessors. He agreed, however, to give their Oxford church twice that number, and chose six older friars, including the local guardian or superior of the friary. To these six, as a gesture of good will, he added the names of the two resident masters of theology. One was Adam Howden, who had just finished his tenure as regent master; the other was Philip of Bridlington, the regent for the coming year. The names of the twelve younger friars, including several bachelors waiting their turn for inception like John Duns, were not given such faculties on that occasion. Apart from being indicative of Bl. John's obvious zeal for the practical ministry, the incident throws considerable light on the fact that John was still assigned to the Oxford friary for the coming school year of 1300-1301, the year of Bridlington's regency. And sometime during that year, we know from the manuscript tradition that he participated as a formed bachelor in one of Master Philip's disputations.

The second incident that occurred was the news of the disastrous defeat of the Sultan of Egypt by the Turks at the battle of Medjamâa-el-Morûdj, December 23, 1299, at the hands of the Turks. Franciscans were especially interested in that event, since their proteges, King Hayton II of Armenia, and Henry II of Cyprus were Christian allies of the Turks. Franciscan emissaries brought the news to Canterbury on June 6, 1300, where it quickly spread to Oxford. There it created great optimism that perhaps the prophecy of Abū Ma'Shar (Albumazar), the leading astronomer in the Muslim world, was being fulfilled. For this Arab's major work on the planets had been translated into Latin (*De Magnis Conjunctionibus*) and was known to Oxford academics. It may well have been in the library Grosseteste left to the Franciscan convent that Roger Bacon first encountered this book when he received the Franciscan habit there some thirty years earlier. "Albumazar says, in the eighth chapter of the second book, the law of Mahomet cannot last more than 693 years," Bacon later wrote in his *Opus Maius*. "Therefore it will be quickly destroyed by the grace of God, which must be a great consolation to Christians."

Duns Scotus may well have expressed this thought in a sermon on the marks of the true church given in the Greyfriars church that summer. Since he had begun work on his *Ordinatio*, the new question he inserted in its Prologue about the sufficiency of the Christian revelation and the superiority of "the law of Christ" to that of the "law of Mahomet" may have been based on what he said in that sermon. At any rate, one remark in the question seems an allusion to both Albumazar's prophecy and the news of the defeat of the Egyptians that awoke such unwarranted optimism in June but was gone before the end of the year. For in citing stability as a mark of the true Church, Scotus asserts: "If the permanence of the sect of Mahomet is cited as an objection, I reply that it began more than six hundred years after the law of Christ and, God willing, it will shortly end, because in this one thousand three hundredth year of Christ it is greatly weakened, and many of its believers have died, and most have fled; and a prophecy among them says that their sect must come to an end" (*Ord.* prol. n. 112).

Scotus' teaching at Cambridge.

By July 1301 John had completed his thirteen years of theological training at Oxford, but needed another year before he could leave for Paris. For that prestigious university required fourteen years of theological training for mendicants coming from abroad (or seven for its own Parisian students), before a bachelor could read the *Sentences* there. John may have gone to Cambridge, for he spent some time teaching there. The colophon, or concluding note, to an early fourteenth-century manuscript in Oxford's Merton College states, "This is from the *Ordinatio* of the Venerable Friar John Duns of the Order of Friars Minor who flourished at Cambridge, Oxford and Paris and died in Cologne."

Scotus' first year in Paris.

John's first year at Paris proved to be an exciting one. To begin with, the city had the greatest of the medieval universities, especially in theological studies. New and important theological problems were being discussed there. It was where great Franciscan teachers like Alexander of Hales or St. Bonaventure had taught, as well as those two great Dominican luminaries, Albert the Great and Thomas Aquinas. With three times the enrollment of Oxford, Paris offered Scotus the chance to meet students and teachers from every place in Europe. It was there that "the Scot" or *Scotus* was added to John's baptismal name, or to his family name of Duns. When Scotus began his lectures in early October 1302, Gonsalvus of Spain was the regent Franciscan master. That year he conducted a famous dispute with the Dominican Meister Eckhart in which Duns Scotus participated.

But even more important political events were stirring in the French capital. The long-standing conflict between Pope Boniface VIII and the French king had come to a head. Feelings were running high and pamphleteers were circulating literature in the Paris streets in favor of the king and demanding the resignation of the pope. The controversy invaded both pulpit and campus; and before Scotus had finished his first year of lectures, the university itself was shut down. How had such a sad state of affairs come about? It began with King Philip the Fair's attempt to extend his territory and political power at the expense of King Edward I of England, who was also Duke of Gascony. War broke out between these two most powerful kings in northern Europe. To finance his war with England, King Philip the Fair began unlawfully to tax church property. Boniface excommunicated him and forbade the University of Paris to grant theological degrees. Philip retaliated by ordering a general council whose avowed intent was to depose the pope. Thus he won over the French clergy, the university, and others to his cause. A great anti-papal demonstration took place on June 24, 1303, in which mendicants (Dominicans and Franciscans) took part. The following day royal commissioners examined each friar to ascertain whether he stood for or against the king. Some seventy friars stood with the king; whereas the rest (approximately eighty) remained loyal to the pope. Among the latter is found the name of John Duns Scotus. According to the royal command, the pope's partisans were to leave France within three days. Scotus and his friend Gonsalvus of Spain, the Franciscan regent master, were among the exiles.

Where Scotus went during his exile is unknown. Perhaps he returned to Oxford, or was this the occasion of his Cambridge lecture? Wherever it might have been, King Philip, meanwhile, had dispatched his henchmen to harass and imprison Boniface, whose death was the result of this experience. Boniface's successor, Benedict XI, in order to restore peace, lifted the ban against Philip and the university in April 1304; royalty reciprocated; and soon the exiles were again studying at the University of Paris.

At the Pentecost Chapter that year, Gonsalvus of Spain became minister general of the Order of Friars Minor. In November he wrote to the guardian at the Paris friary that he was appointing as the next regent master of theology "Friar John Scotus, of whose laudable life, excellent knowledge and most subtle ability, as well as his other remarkable qualities I am fully informed, partly from long experience and partly from report which has spread everywhere." Tradition tells us that Scotus, sometime during his sojourn in Paris, gave a brilliant defense of the Immaculate Conception of the Blessed Virgin Mary, and it may be this that brought him fame and to which Gonsalvus refers.

Scotus' regency in Paris

Scotus became master sometime early the next year (1305). As regent he would have had the task of explaining some book of the Bible in his early morning lectures and conducting an occasional "ordinary disputation" in which bachelors might participate as opponents and respondents. We know that Scotus did conduct one such ordinary disputation with the Dominican master, Godin, on what constitutes the principle of individuation. There were also vigorous controversies between Duns and the Dominican master Hervé de Nédellac. John's striking defense of the Immaculate Conception aroused the animosity of the secular master, Jean de Pouilly, as we can infer from the latter's *Quodlibet* of 1308. Besides these public disputations, Scotus must have also held other less formal discussions with students in the Franciscan friary at Paris, just as he had in Oxford, for the collection of theological questions known as *Collationes* are from both his Oxford and Paris periods. There is some evidence that he may have also discussed some logical and metaphysical questions for the benefit of students beginning their studies at the university, since one of his younger disciples, Antonius Andreas, introduces two of his logical works with the observation that its contents are based on what he was able to gather "from the statements of the Master John Duns, of the Scottish nation, sitting in magisterial chair." Teachers customarily impart their wisdom orally rather than attempt to put it into writing for posterity, and this was obviously true in the case of what Scotus taught. It should not surprise us, then, that the manuscripts that have come down to us from the early fourteenth century contain nothing of his university sermons or his biblical lectures. No, the major publishing project for Scotus, and one in which his secretaries were still engaged at the Paris friary, was his monumental *Ordinatio*, based on his Oxford and Parisian lectures on the *Sentences*. This, like the revision of his great magisterial *Quodlibet*, was still unfinished when he had to leave the French capital for Cologne. And it is on these two works, rather than his writings on Aristotle's philosophy, that his great fame as a philosopher and theologian depends. And it is in these two works that we must look for the blueprints to the theological cathedral that Pope Paul VI so admired as the work of this intellectual giant.

Quodlibets

Earlier we spoke of his Sentence-commentary, which came to be known as his Oxford work. Here it may be appropriate to add some remarks about his *Quodlibet*, which was the major contribution to theology as a regent master in Paris. "Quodlibet" is the Latin term for "anything." And a digression on this special sort of disputation "where anything goes" is perhaps in order here.

Few works of the medieval scholastics were written in the style of present day books. They were rather collections of questions that were raised in the course of some public debate or disputation. From his earliest years the theological student had been coached in debating under the supervision of a master in that art. At the beginning of his studies, the student was introduced to the questions which he would need later; then he was trained both to learn to defend his solution to the problem or "question" and to raise difficulties against a particular solution. It will be remembered that part of the course included the official answering of objections to a particular question and also the official proposing of objections to solutions given. The less formal, or "private," disputations were those which a teacher or lecturer held in his own quarters or study house. Duns Scotus' theological *Collationes*, we referred to above, may be the result of such disputations. In contrast to this were the variety of public disputations bachelors or masters engaged in. "Ordinary" disputations (also called "solemn" or "public") consisted in a master's disputing on fixed days of the week for more than just his own students. There were the disputations on the eve of the granting of the doctorate in theology ("vesperies") and on the day itself, called the "inception" or the "aula" disputation in which the candidate disputed before the bishop in the main hall of the university (aula). But the most solemn disputations were the *Quodlibets* held by the regent masters.

These quodlibetals were like the presidential news conferences or the public debates between the candidates for the presidency of the United States where "anything" (*quodlibet*) can be asked by "anyone" (*quolibet*) and usually is. A master could hold such a solemn disputation either during Advent or during Lent. Ordinarily in the quodlibetals, several pro and con preliminary presentations would be made by bachelors. But once the master took over, it was any question on any subject. Anyone could be present for these quodlibetals—master, student, visitor, or whoever wished. And all were free to ask any question whatever, so long as it was of current interest. The master, however, could refuse questions which had no meaning or were of minor import. In the light of what could be asked, it is hardly surprising that some masters refused to conduct such a quodlibetal disputation, since such was a formidable test of presence of mind, intellectual ability, and wide experience. Since the questions raised usually covered a variety of topics and, in the course of the disputation itself, did not follow one another in any particular order, it was customary for a master to arrange them later in some orderly fashion before releasing them for public distribution.

During his brief regency Scotus held but one such quodlibetal disputation. The twenty two questions that were brought up during its course, he rearranged under the general heading of "God and Creatures." Since the final question was only partially revised, we may conclude that this work, the revision of his *Ordinatio*, was unfinished on the eve of his sudden departure for Cologne, and it was left to his secretarial staff to complete these two most important of his theological writings with portions taken from the reports (*reportata*) that were jotted down by scribes during the actual lecture or disputation.

Scotus' lectorship in Cologne

His sudden departure from Paris in 1307 for the city of Cologne, where he lectured at the friary on theology, has an air of mystery about it. Scotus is at the height of his career! Was it that some considered his views on the Immaculate Conception heretical? Or was it to forestall Scotus' incurring the king's enmity for opposing Philip's attempt to have the master general of the Knights Templar declared a heretic, and on the suppression of the Templars, to confiscate the Order's wealth for his royal treasury? Was it simply that there was a need to share his learning with other houses of the Order?

Scotus' death

Whatever may have been the reason for his transfer to Cologne, on November 8, 1308, after forty-two years and a glorious career as Scot, Franciscan, possibly the greatest metaphysician of the Middle Ages, and surely an architect "the pinnacles of whose temple reached to the heavens," the Subtle Doctor breathed his last. The mortal remains of John Duns Scotus now rest in an ornate sarcophagus in the nave of the Conventual Minoritenkirche near the Cologne cathedral where he is venerated as a saint. Among the many who have prayed at his tomb was Pope John Paul II, who officially recognized his cult "from time immemorial." This means Blessed John Duns Scotus is beatified, with November 8th as his traditional feast day.

Part III

THE TEMPLE

From the splendid theological temple Scotus has raised next to that of Aquinas, we select some key foundation stones that are distinctively Scotistic. Archbishop H. E. Cardinale, Apostolic Delegate to Great Britain, pointed them out in his inaugural address in the Church of St. Mary the Virgin Oxford that officially opened the Second International Scotistic Congress on September 11, 1966. For many reasons it was a particularly momentous occasion, the first since the Protestant Reformation, when a Catholic prelate stood in the pulpit of this venerable Oxford church that had been the "center of the life of the University from its earliest infancy, [where] young students and their professors would assemble for worship as well as for academic exercises." Cardinale considered it especially fitting that "the Congress honoring John Duns Scotus should be inaugurated in a church dedicated to the Blessed Mother of God, of whose Immaculate Conception, as a logical corollary to his Doctrine of the Primacy of Christ, he was the intrepid and strenuous defender, in direct opposition to the greatest scholars of his time and six centuries before the definition of the dogma." The Congress itself was a long "overdue act of reparation to the distorted memory of one of the greatest sons of Oxford," the city to which Thomas Cromwell sent a Cambridge priest, Richard Layton, "to destroy all documents and books pertaining to Scotus and to proscribe his teachings, though they were *not a foreign imposition, but had been brought to flower on the fertile soil of his fatherland.*" What a senseless holocaust that burning of those precious manuscripts in the quad seems to us today when "the many and heterogeneous works of Scotus offer numberless elements for a fruitful study and meditation, likely to be welcomed by our contemporary world. For all its distractions, our present generation," Cardinale pointed out, "feels the need of a new intellectual synthesis, in which to retrieve the final answers to the questions that anguish its mind."

The theme Cardinale chose for his address was titled "The Significance of the Apostolic Letter *Alma Parens* of Pope Paul VI," the first official papal document dedicated to the teachings of Scotus since his predecessor Paul V in 1610 decreed that "whatever appeared to belong to Scotus, was to be kept intact and inviolate."

SCOTUS' NOTION OF THE INDIVIDUAL

Alma Parens pointed out that "Saint Francis of Assisi's most beautiful ideal of perfection and the ardor of the Seraphic Spirit are embedded in the work of Scotus and inflame it." It is this point that Cardinale would like to explain. Though he wishes to concentrate on Scotus more as a theologian, he cannot resist the temptation of putting him into relation with modern thought, and the first key philosophical notion that he singles out is precisely the one that throws light on our problem.

> In the philosophical system of Scotus the individual reigns supreme against the general trend of his age which gave pride of place to the universal and relegated the individual to the domain of the accidental and the perishable. Medieval man thought and lived within the orbit of a deep collective consciousness; he was absorbed into a strong social structure where he easily lost awareness of his individuality and personal responsibility. Reacting to the common trend, St. Francis of Assisi emphasized the importance of the individual in his rule, leaving much to the inspiration and guidance of divine grace. Scotus who translated into metaphysical language "the most beautiful Franciscan ideal of perfection and the ardor of the Seraphic spirit" bases this integration on the principle of differentiation and individuation.

St. Francis respected each and every individual God had created in a special way. It was a respect that was independent of what they were, or what virtues or merits each possessed. It was not only in the leper that Francis discovered Christ, but in each and every human being. "Realize the dignity God has conferred on you," he admonished his friars, "He created and formed your body in the image of his beloved Son, and your soul in his own likeness." Nor was it only persons that he reverenced in this way but everything that had tumbled from the creative hand of God. Each was either a "brother" or a "sister" to him. How did Scotus "translate into metaphysical language" this reverential insight of Francis?

He did it, as Cardinale correctly observes, through his "principle of differentiation and individuation." The principle of individuation was a philosophical problem Scotus discussed many times, for it had created a special problem for theology in his day. His age, as Cardinale points out, "gave pride of place to the universal and relegated the individual to the domain of the accidental and the perishable." This was the pre-Christian philosophical view of the Greek philosopher Aristotle, whose conception of the universe was rediscovered when the universities were born and became the basis for their liberal arts program. Known in university circles simply as "The Philosopher," Aristotle stressed the importance of mind over matter, of the intellect over sense perception, of the universal over the singular or particular. It is the ability of the mind, the intellect, to grasp the common features, characteristics and properties of the material world about us. Consider our encounter with something new, seen for the first time. What do we know about it? How do we describe it? It is always in terms of something familiar, some feature, some aspect that we have seen or encountered before, some property that this individual item shares with another. All our descriptive terms, in short, are common nouns, adjectives or verbs. They are applied, or at least can apply, to more than one; in fact—logically speaking—we see no reason to limit the number to which the term might be applied. But each individual precisely as individual has something of its own, over and above the nature or properties it may share with others. We call this its individuality.

The philosophical problem of individuation

Just what is this individuality? its precise nature? its source? its relationship to the common properties an individual shares with others? Philosophers, since the time of Plato and Aristotle, have puzzled over an adequate answer. Aristotle's explanation was in terms of matter and form, a distinction he borrowed from the world of art. An artifact is said to be composed of matter and form. A potter, for instance, gives a form to the clay or matter he uses, and this matter becomes an artistic vase, an ornamental urn, a useful goblet, a cooking pot. One can duplicate, or replicate the form again and again, so long as there is material to receive it. It is the amount or quantity of the material, whatever it may be, that determines the number of individual vessels that can be made. Form seems to become tied down, limited, or individualized through the matter that receives it, and matter in turn seems limited either of itself, or by reason of its quantity or extension. Aristotle generalized this idea, equating the essence or nature of any material substance with what he called its "substantial form," and making the material or its quantitative aspect his principle of individuation.

Aquinas adopted this conception of Aristotle, at least in regard to material things. Pure spirits, like the angels which have no matter, differ from one another specifically, not as individuals. The human soul as spiritual is individuated by its relationship with the material body which it informs. The Order of Preachers had made Thomas Aquinas their "common doctor"; and we recall that Scotus, as regent master conducted a disputation with the Dominican Peter Godin as to whether matter was the principle of individuation. Matter itself, Scotus argued, needs a source or principle of individuation. This cannot be done by something accidental to a material substance, like quantity. Furthermore, he saw no reason why God could not make two angels of the same kind, without making them specifically different from one another. Neither did most of the other theologians at the university who were suspicious of the orthodoxy of this particular theory of individuation.

Scotus' solution

It would not do to deny there was a problem, or to claim all things are simply individual to begin with, and differ from each other as individuals, and that is that. This would mean that individuals do not share common features, and all our scientific knowledge based on such universal properties is simply wrong. Furthermore, there would be no degrees of difference. Plato would be no more like Socrates than he would be like a stone or distant star. No, if our intellectual knowledge is objective, those shared features our mind perceives to be in things must really be in each one; but if the feature is such as can be shared, then neither it nor any combination of such explains its individuality. Something more is needed, some positive additive.

What could this positive principle be? Scotus carefully examined each answer his contemporaries proposed. One suggested it might be existence in the real world that individuates a nature, since no idea can be realized in the actual world without becoming individual. Scotus, however, argued that existence is logically distinct from and something in addition to the individual's individuality. God conceived of Adam and Eve as two individuals even before he gave them existence. Matter and quantity are not ultimate answers either, particularly where something spiritual or immaterial in nature, like the human soul or an angelic nature, is concerned. The individuating principle must be in the soul itself, intrinsic to it as such, not just a relationship it has to a material body. And angels have no matter, even if it be of an ectoplasmic or quasi-spiritual sort. Hence, he argued that in each individual there is an individuating difference which is unique and proper to that individual. It is what makes it this, and not that. "This" and "that" are indexical terms, philosophers of language tell us. We use them to point to what we cannot describe. Since *haec* is the Latin term for "this," Scotus and his disciples referred to this positive additive that individuates generically as "haecceity" (*haecceitas*) or "thisness." But haecceity, like individuality, is a universal, a common term, and it does not really tells us what a particular individual's individuality really is. It only describes its twofold function: (1) To make that individual unique and incapable of duplication, even by an omnipotent God; and (2) to differentiate it from each and every other individual, whether it be of the same or a specifically different type.

Is haecceity knowable?

If each individual's haecceity is intrinsically different from that of any other individual's, can it be known? Not if by "known" we mean "conceptualized," for all our intellectual concepts are universal, whereas any given individuating difference is what philosophers call the individual's "bare particularity." Where other individuals are concerned, we know them to be different, and distinguish one from another, not in terms of their individuating haecceity, but in terms of what descriptive properties they may have that others do not. But if haecceity is something positive, it should be knowable to God, at least, who created it. And there is one instance where each one of us is aware of individuality, namely, the introspective recognition of our self. "I" or "Me" are proper names we give that self. "My" is the adjectival word that joins to that bare, particular, subject-self, whatever I know or can conceive about it. In any true statement I make about myself, such as "I exist...," "I doubt...," "I feel...," or the like, implies as a pre-condition for its verity, an intuitive awareness of my individuality, my bare particularity. I recognize its identity from day to day. I may lose sight of it in my absorption in what is about me, for I am object oriented, concerned with my surroundings. I may blank it from consciousness completely when I fall asleep. But on awakening I find it has returned, the same "I" remembered from the time before I fell asleep, the same "I" that yesterday was me. All else "about me," may have changed, be it the ambient world, or what I see, feel, or introspect about my self. But my individuality remains undivided in itself, distinct from everything other than itself. It is that to which the terms "I" and "Me" refer.

God too knows my haecceity, for was it not he who created it? And he also knows the individuality of each and every person or thing around me, though I at present do not. But this brings another thought to mind. One that gives a spiritual dimension and orientation to Scotus' otherwise abstract theory of individuating differences.

Haecceity, our personal gift from God

If we reflect on this Scotistic conception of individuality in the context of what he believes God to be, we discover it means that God's creative love wanted just this person or this creature to exist, rather than its twin or perfect copy. When we ponder this more deeply, we see it invests each individual with a special value, quite apart from the type or sort of thing it may be. God could have substituted another individual with precisely the same nature, properties or abilities as he gave this individual. There is a replaceable part, so to speak, for each one us. But when we realize God did not use that replacement but chose us instead, that can give us a more profound sense of where our real worth lies in the eyes of God—a realization that can be both psychologically comforting, but may have a sobering effect as well. One the one hand, for a person psychologically despondent or depressed, it can be the source of a fresh sense of personal value, for as long as God gives one existence, it means one is still a special object of God's continued creative love. For the repentant sinner, this can be an indestructible foundation for renewed hope. On the other hand, it can have a salutary sobering effect, for it makes us realize that whatever nature or talents we have, they are something apart from what makes us unique and singular, for God could have duplicated anything we have or are in another individual, one who might have made better use of such talents or abilities than we, regrettably, did.

Social implications

Cardinale in his explanation of the significance of *Alma Parens* goes on to show how this appreciation of the value of "the human person as an individual" is like a leitmotif that runs through "every phase of his system."

This is true of Scotus' social and economic philosophy as well, for as Cardinale notes:

> His reflections are not restricted to the metaphysical order: he even gives amazing new and revolutionary glimpses into the social theories of the last three centuries. In his writings we can trace the beginnings of modern political and social science. Political authority, according to Scotus, may belong both to a single person or to the community as a whole; but in either case the legitimate sanction of authority is derived from the consent of the individuals who are governed.

In short, no human being has an any "divine right" to rule over any other adult, whatever be that individual's social status. Much less has any one individual the right to exploit another, or one nation of individuals to exploit a less developed country for its own aggrandizement. "By this exaltation of the human person with its psychological autonomy and basic rights," Cardinale points out, "Scotus at the very outset takes his stand against all totalitarian systems."

Are individuals necessary for the order in the universe?

It is interesting to note that after his detailed discussion of the principle of individuation in which he submitted every rival theory proposed by his contemporaries to searching criticism, Scotus raises the question of whether there can be several angels in the same species. We briefly referred above to Aquinas's theory that angels are not technically individuals. That is to say, though singular, one does not differ from the other by an individuating difference but rather by one that is specific. Each angel, for St. Thomas, represented a species. This followed from the fact that the angels as pure spirits lacked matter or any quantitative characteristics that material bodies possess, if one accepted as Aquinas did Aristotle's theory of individuation.

Antiquated or as irrelevant to modern interests as this conception may seem to us today, it does have some implications as to whether individuals are really necessary for the order God had in mind in creating the universe. The order that pervades the universe is what makes it a thing of beauty, a cosmos. But order is based on specific differences. There is no order, no priority or posteriority, among individuals as individuals. To know all the various species or types of things that make up the cosmos might pertain to perfection of knowledge. But where individuals are concerned, as the saying goes, "when you have seen one, you have seen all." Consequently, some of the Islamic philosophers, influenced by Aristotle, questioned whether God had, or needed, any knowledge of individuals, since individuality seemed to add nothing conceptually to what can be known of individuals intellectually. God's knowledge, they argued, would be no less perfect if restricted to a knowledge of each species.

Obviously Aquinas or those like him who believed that each angel had only specific perfection, not individuality, could not, and did not, as Christians, believe this true of God. But they did use a similar argument in favor of their philosophical view of angels. "Numerical plurality is not something intended by nature," they claimed, "for the intent of nature is satisfied and rests essentially in those beings which pertain to the order of the universe. In angels, however, there is nothing that does not pertain to the order and beauty of the universe. Therefore, in angels there is not numerical difference." (*Ordinatio* II, 3, 7, n. 220) This was a possible objection to his theory that Scotus felt he ought to answer.

In reply he reminded his objectors of St. Augustine's definition of order in *The City of God.* "Order is an arrangement of like and unlike things whereby each is disposed to its proper place." That is why Scotus went on say, our creator,

> who primarily intended the order of the universe (as the principal good, intrinsic to himself) not only intended this inequality that is one requirement for order (among species), but also desired a parity of individuals (within the same species), which is another accompaniment of order. And individuals are intended in an unqualified sense by this 'First One' insofar as he intended something other than himself not as an end, but as something oriented to that end. Hence to communicate his goodness, as something befitting his beauty, he produces several in each species. And in those beings which are the highest and most important, it is the individual that is primarily intended by God (n. 252).

To fully appreciate the value of the individual, Scotus is telling us here, one must consider what God "primarily intended" when he made "those beings which are the highest and most important"—persons, gifted with intellect and will, like ourselves and choirs of angels.

But just what does he mean in speaking of this "order" as "intrinsic to himself" and that we, as "other than God," are intended not as an end "but as something ordered to that end"? To understand the profound implications of what he puts so succinctly here, we must study more carefully what he considered God to be and what he thought might be God's "motive" in creating.

SCOTUS' CONCEPTION OF GOD

In *Alma Parens* Pope Paul VI recalls how Scotus "built up his theodicy from the scriptural principles regarding God," namely, Exodus 3:14 where God gave as his name "*I am who am*," and 1 John 4:16 where we find him described simply as "*God is love*."

Proof of God's existence

Scotus did construct one of the most elaborate and ingenious versions of the cosmological argument for God's existence in the history of philosophy. Its philosophical foundations were metaphysical, the fruit of John's earlier studies in the liberal arts of the metaphysics of Aristotle, especially as interpreted by Avicenna, the Persian savant known to his Islamic co-religionists by his Arabic name of Ibn Sina. He incorporated into the proof all the valid basic insights of earlier scholastic proofs but wove them together into a closely knit, logically consistent whole that revealed God as a supreme being as infinite in nature. As Cardinale points out:

> His argumentation rests on the contingency and mutability of creatures, which imply a chain of causation, resulting ultimately in the First Cause, whose nature is infinite and perfect. His rigid demands of the qualifications required to prove a proposition make his arguments all the more attractive to the modern mind.

The detailed nature of the proof, a small book in itself, can be fully appreciated only through a prolonged and careful study. Unfortunately we cannot present it appropriately in this present work. But Scotus, with the aid of one of his disciples, made an extract of the proof from the *Ordinatio* in a prayerful treatise entitled *De Primo Principio* (i.e., about God as First Principle), from which we extract two paragraphs. The first (§1.2) is this prayer with which Scotus begins the treatise.

> May the First Principle of things grant me to believe, to understand, and to reveal what may please his majesty and may raise our minds to contemplate him. O Lord our God, true teacher that you are, when Moses your

servant asked you for your name that he might proclaim it to the children of Israel, you, knowing what the mind of mortals could grasp of you, replied: "I am who am," thus disclosing your blessed name. You are truly what it means to be, you are the whole of what it means to exist. This, if it should be possible for me, I should like to know by way of demonstration. Help me, then, O Lord, as I investigate how much natural reason can learn about that true being which you are if we begin with the being which you have predicated of yourself.

The second item is his summation of what he believes he has proved as a philosopher and metaphysician.

O Lord, our God, Catholics can infer most of the perfections which philosophers knew of you from what has been said. You are the first efficient cause, the ultimate end, supreme in perfection, transcending all things. You are uncaused in any way and therefore incapable of becoming or perishing, indeed it is simply impossible that you should not exist, for of yourself you are necessary being. You are therefore eternal, because the span of your existence is without limit and you experience it all at once, for it cannot be strung out in a succession of events. For there can be no succession save in what is continually caused, or at least in what is dependent for its existence upon another, and this dependence is a far cry from what has necessary being of itself. You live a most noble life, because you are understanding and volition. You are happy, indeed you are by nature happiness itself, because you are in possession of yourself. You are the clear vision of yourself and the most joyful love, and although you are self-sufficient and happy in yourself alone, you still understand in a single act everything that can be known. At one and the same time you possess the power to freely and contingently will each thing that can be caused and, by willing it through your volition, cause it to be. Most truly then you are of infinite power. You are incomprehensible, infinite, for nothing omniscient or of infinite power is finite...Neither is the ultimate end, nor what exists of itself in all simplicity, something finite. Your are the ultimate in simplicity, having no really distinct parts, or no realities in your essence which are not really the same. In you no quantity, no accident can be found, and therefore you are incapable of accidental change, even as I have already expressed, you are so in essence. You alone are simply perfect, not just a perfect angel or a perfect body, but a perfect being, lacking no entity it is possible for anything to have. Nothing can formally possess every perfection, but every entity can exist in something either formally or eminently, as it does in you, O God, who are supreme among beings, the only one of them who is infinite. Communicating the rays of your goodness most liberally, you are boundless good to whom as the most lovable thing of all every single being in its own way comes back to you as to its ultimate end. (*A Treatise on God as First Principle*, §4.84).

Small wonder then that Pope Paul VI confessed: "We are deeply convinced that the valuable theological treasure of John Duns Scotus can provide formidable weapons in the struggle to disperse the black cloud of atheism which hangs darkly over our age.''

A work Scotus planned but never lived to write

In *A Treatise on God as First Principle*, Scotus tells us, addressing himself to God:

> I have tried to show how the metaphysical properties affirmed of you can be inferred in some way by natural reason. In the tract that follows, those shall be set forth that are the subject of belief, wherein reason is held captive—yet to Catholics, the latter are more certain since they rest firmly on your own most solid truth and not upon our intellect which is blind and weak in many things.

Unfortunately for us, John did not live long enough to finish this second treatise, a companion volume on wonderful things we know of God because of divine revelation. But we are not left completely in the dark as to what this second treatise might be like. For he would undoubtedly have selected from his theological works what he had written about God as ''omnipotent, immense, omnipresent, just, yet merciful, provident of all creatures but looking after intellectual ones in a special way.'' And it is to some of the more striking theological conceptions Scotus had of God and of his motive in creation we now turn. These can be shown to grow out of the second scriptural text Pope Paul VI quotes as basic to Scotus' theology, namely, ''God is love,'' just as the metaphysical treatise on the First Principle grew out of God's description of himself as ''I am who am.''

The trinity that is God

If the latter description led Scotus to a conception of God as one unique infinite being, whose perfections he spelled out so profusely in the citation above, what might he have inferred from the fact that God is love? For like St. Bonaventure, a generation before him, Scotus was both familiar with and impressed by the insights of Richard of St. Victor as to what that might imply. Richard was a monk of the Abbey of St. Victor in the outskirts of Paris. There each day in choir the Athanasian creed was recited, praising those divine attributes shared equally by Father, Son, and Holy Spirit.

> . . . we worship one God in trinity and trinity in unity. Neither confounding the persons, nor dividing the substance. For there is one person of the Father, another of the Son, and another of the Holy Spirit. But the Godhead of the Father, of the Son and of the Holy Spirit is all one, the glory equal, the majesty co-eternal.

So the solemn chant rang out each day in the vaulted choir of the abbey church. Each day Richard heard the words resound:

Such as the Father is, such is the Son, and such is the Holy Spirit. The Father uncreated, the Son uncreated, and the Holy Spirit uncreated. The Father incomprehensible, the Son incomprehensible, and the Holy Spirit incomprehensible. The Father is eternal, the Son is eternal, and the Holy Spirit is eternal and yet they are not three eternals but one eternal. As also there are not three uncreated, nor three incompehensibles, but one uncreated, and one incomprehensible. So likewise the Father is almighty, the Son almighty, and the Holy Spirit almighty. And yet they are not three almighties but one almighty . . .

As a teacher of the young men who came to the abbey school for instruction, Richard of St. Victor puzzled how this central mystery of our faith might somehow be explained. How could God be both three and one? One day as the monks' profound profession of faith rose from their choir stalls to the vaulted ceiling the answer came to Richard. If God is love, as St. John tells us, then that love must be in God most perfect. Perfect love, Richard reflected, is not jealous or envious, but seeks co-lovers for what is loved. Like an artist who has created a breathtaking painting, or sculptor who has carved a splendid statue, or the patron who has procured a priceless work of art, each desires to put that treasure on display, to share its radiant loveliness with others. But the mutual admiration between two persons alone is not enough, Richard argued in his great work *On the Trinity*. Three at least are needed before love can be perfect. For the love that links any two is itself something so good, so beautiful, so precious, that it must be shared with another. Love is multiple, yet unifies. That is what the mystery of the Trinity reveals.

Motive for creation

This Victorine idea of what a God of love must be like intrigued two great Franciscan thinkers; first St. Bonaventure, who used it to explain not only the inner life of the Trinity, but why everything that tumbled from God's creative hands bore trinitarian fingerprints. And a generation later, Duns Scotus employed it to explain why creation would have been incomplete, as it were, had God not created co-lovers as well.

The manner in which the two Franciscans applied the Victorine principle, however, was somewhat different. Scotus did not try to use it directly to provide some kind of rational explanation for the trinity of persons. Rather for this purpose he concentrated on the fact that if, as theologians generally believed, the divine procession of one person from another or others would involve either the divine intellect or the divine will, then the persons generated or spirated would be limited to two. This, together with the idea that the Father is primarily unbegotten, though "productive," implied that the number of persons would be three. St. Bonaventure, admitting that Richard's argumentation fell short of being a purely rational demonstration, nevertheless regarded it as a reasonably persuasive argument for a pluraliy of persons. But he went farther than Richard, who used his argument to establish the simple fact that a plurality of persons was needed for perfect love, and the minimal number for such was three. The Franciscan saint sought to explain why the nature communicated would be the same for each person. Thus Bonaventure argued as follows:

> Suppose there is in God supreme happiness. Wherever there is supreme happiness, however, there is supreme goodness, supreme charity and supreme enjoyment as well. But if there is supreme goodness, since it is characteristic of goodness to communicate itself supremely and this is especially in producing from itself an equal and giving its own being, [then it follows in God this would occur]. If there is supreme charity, since charity is not private love, but is directed to another, it therefore requires a plurality of persons. Likewise, if there is supreme enjoyment, since there is not enjoyable possession of a good without a companion, therefore for supreme enjoyment companionship is required and hence a plurality of persons. (*I Sent.* d. 2, art. un., q. 2)

Here we see Bonaventure combining the Richardian principle with that of pseudo-Dionysius that goodness is *self-diffusive*. Not only would there be a plurality of persons if God was love, but if God was good, their procession from one another whereby the divine nature is communicated from the Father to the Son, and with and through the Son to the Holy Spirit, would have this result. Each would have the same being as the other, and in the case of God, since there can be but one God, each would have the same individual being as the other, for there is but one God.

It was this last argument that Scotus objected to. God indeed is one, but this is what the Dionysian principle as used by Bonaventure jeopardizes. For, if the divine good was supremely communicative, this would imply that it produced another with the same being as itself. Scotus questioned whether the mystery of why three persons had but one divine nature could be so readily explained. Even when Christ revealed that God is triune, we can only accept this as an article of faith; we cannot hope to understand it as pilgrims here on earth. The most we can conclude from the Dionysian principle that good is self-diffusive and God is supreme goodness, would be that divine goodness would tend to diffusive itself in a superlative fashion, but not that it would produce another with the identical being that it had. The snag Scotus saw here is that the productive/product relationship is one that sets up a polar opposition between the two terms, a real distinction between producer and what is produced. We admit such a distinction between the divine persons, but not between the divine nature they share in common. In fact, one of Scotus' proofs for the unicity of God was the fact that a good, if infinite, could not be duplicated, or—to assume the impossible—if replication is possible, there is no intrinsic reason why it would be limited to any finite number. It would follow, then, that it could be replicated *ad infinitum*, and since in the case of an infinite or all-perfect good, it could not be caused, then its very possibility would entail actuality. Thus one would have to conclude that if the divine nature was supremely diffusive and as such produced a perfect likeness to its own being, an actual infinity of gods would exist—something no philosopher would concede.

Scotus, therefore, argues that if one wishes to apply the self-diffusive characteristic of goodness to productivity in God, it would explain something about creation rather than about how the divine nature is communicated to the divine persons. So interpreted, the Dionysian principle might account for the astounding variety of what God has created, something scientists have been studying for centuries and will go on exploring as long as humankind exists on earth. If God's perfections are infinite but can only be communicated in a finite degree and therefore in piecemeal fashion, we would expect an unusually lavish display and endless diversity such as we see unfolding before our eyes as we explore the constituents of systems within systems that make up our many-layered cosmos.

But here Scotus exploits Richard's principle in a ingenious way that Bonaventure does not envision. For—as we noted earlier—Scotus was impressed not only by the wonderful variety of species that make up the order of the universe, but with the importance of each individual within the species, since each was chosen particularly by God. And he argued there, we recall, that not only did the individual pertain essentially to the order of the universe, but where the higher species of creatures were concerned, it was each individual that was intended in a special way by God rather than the fact that one such instance of that species existed. God, in short, wanted many created individual co-lovers of what the Trinity of persons loved in a special way.

The will as the power to love

Richard's analysis of perfect love regarded this affection primarily if not exclusively as an action. Scotus, however, as a philosopher was also concerned with the power or root source of that action, the will. For, as Cardinale pointed out in his explanation of the *Alma Parens* to fully understand Scotus' "exaltation of the human person with its psychological autonomy and basic rights" it is also necessary to consider

> his fundamental doctrine on the will, the primary faculty in his system and
> on the pre-eminence of love over knowledge. The freedom of the will is an

indispensable complement to personality, and since love pertains to the will, the whole creation is seen as a work of love on God's part.

SCOTUS' NOTION OF THE WILL

Let us first consider Scotus' conception of the will as it applies first to ourselves and then as it must exist in God, for only then shall we be able to appreciate the grandeur of Scotus' theological synthesis. Theologians in his day had long associated this faculty in rational creatures with their ability to love what is good and attain what is useful in an intelligent fashion. Since Aristotle's philosophy had become commonplace in the universities as the basis of the liberal arts program, they sought to fit the will and its ability to choose somehow into his conceptual framework. A subject's abilities or potentialities were referred to as potencies, and in the case of human nature these were classified in various ways, for instance, as active or, if receptive, as passive. Active potencies, depending on whether or not they were guided by reason or intelligence, were in turn divided into rational or irrational respectively. Where rational potencies were concerned, Aristotle indicated that choice or a freedom to select alternatives entered in. Unlike the scholastic theologians, however, he never spoke of "will" (or *voluntas*) as a special rational potency distinct from the intellect. The Latins also designated the source of any striving or seeking as an appetite (*appetitus*). As an active potency or power to love what is good in an intelligent way, the will could be and often was defined simply as an intellective or rational appetite.

There is an important philosophical difference between Duns Scotus and Thomas Aquinas here, however. Where Aquinas was content to accept this as an adequate description in terms of an Aristotelian-Platonic action-theory, Scotus believed it only indicated the generic aspect of the will, not its specific difference as free. To understand fully the nature of the will's freedom, he felt we must draw upon certain seminal ideas of the will and its freedom he discovered in St. Anselm of Canterbury, sometimes called the "Father of Scholasticism." One was Anselm's positive description of the will's freedom, the other was his proof that if the will were only an intellective appetite it would not be free to sin.

St. Anselm's definition of free will

Many theologians were content to describe free will as it existed in a human or angelic nature as a power to sin. But surely this did not do justice to this power that angels or human beings possess as rational agents. It stresses what is imperfect about this faculty or power, not its perfection; it describes its weakness rather than its strength. What is more, if will or its freedom is so defined, then volition or free will cannot be ascribed to God.

Yet Scripture tells us the blessed sing praise before the throne of God: "For you have created all things: by your will they came to be and were made!" (Rv 4:11) Whatever is to be said about the divine nature, or inner life of the divine persons, creation on the part of God was not a necessary action, something the divine nature required for its own perfection or self-fulfilment. If creation proceeded from the divine nature or Godhead by some necessary emanation process as some of the pagan philosophers believed, there would be no contingency in the world, Scotus argued. Neither could we explain our personal experience of freedom or responsibility for what we will or nill.

How define free will positively? This was the question a disciple of St. Anselm presented to his teacher. The theological context in which the question arose was in connection with the fall of the devil and the sin of our first parents whereby they lost the original state of rectitude or justice that God had given them. They chose to disobey God's command, not out of any necessity of nature, but deliberately and freely because they loved something in a sinful way, rather than justly in the way God wished it to be willed or nilled. But if they sinned by making a bad choice, did they not also have the power to choose correctly? And had they elected to do what was right, they would have made the proper decision, that dictated by right reason, and in so doing have remained in the state of rectitude or justice in which God had created them. If so, should not free will be defined in positive terms of what it could and was able to do? in terms of what it should do and what it would have been right and just to do?

With this in mind St. Anselm defined his free will as Adam's "power to preserve rectitude of will for the sake of that rectitude itself." When the will chooses freely in accord with right reason, then it remains upright; it preserves its rectitude; it does justice both to itself and to what it chooses. If this is the nature of free will, then the will must have an inclination to act in this way, an "affection for justice" (*affectio iustitiae*), Anselm called it. Scotus, we know, accepted this Anselmian description of freedom, and went on to define the will in terms of what this implied.

But in creatures, there is also a God-given natural inclination to perfect themselves, to love and to seek what is necessary or advantageous, and when this drive is satisfied, it brings with it a contentment, a happiness. This natural inclination Anselm called an "affection for the beneficial or advantageous" (*affectio commodi*), and in rational creatures, like angelic or human beings, such an inclination could be attributed to the will as well to the sense appetites.

The twofold affection of the will

As Scotus points out, according to Anselm, the will has a twofold inclination towards what is good, an affection for justice and an affection for the beneficial. As free, it can choose in accord with either inclination, and when it makes a choice it will be in accord with one or the other of these inclinations. The affection for justice, however, is the higher and more perfect of the two. For the affection for the advantageous only seeks a good as a means to a further end which, in turn, is desired for its own sake. The affection for justice, by contrast, always seeks a thing *for its own sake*. That is to say, it tends towards that end in a special way. For it seeks to do justice to its intrinsic worth, its objective value. In another respect, the inclination for justice is superior to the affection the will has for what is advantageous. The latter inclination can be immoderate, especially as regards those things that pertain to one's own welfare and happiness. The affection for justice, however, is never intemperate, inordinate or unreasonable, and even when directed toward one's self is never an exaggerated self-love, but always in accord with right reason. And where God is concerned or the welfare of loved ones or the community is at stake, the affection for justice can transcend self-interest, and be truly unselfish and altruistic. Both these affections can be directed to God, and in loving him they find their most complete fulfilment. One inclines us to love God because he is our good; the other because he is good and lovable in himself. From a supernatural viewpoint, the theological virtue of hope perfects the will's inclination for the advantageous whereas that of charity perfects its affection for justice.

Because St. Anselm developed his theory of the will's twofold inclination in a work entitled *The Fall of the Devil*, the "justice" or state of rectitude he had in mind, pertained primarily to the supernatural order. It is what theologians would later refer to as "sanctifying grace" that elevates and supernaturalizes human nature, as it were, and insofar as it affects the will, is identified with the infused theological virtue of charity. But however one conceives of God's grace, whether it be an entity existing in the soul, or a special relationship which God freely enters into with his creation, it is not something any creature demands or requires by reason of its natural perfection. The very word "grace" means a freely given gift rather than a payment of what is due or owed in strict justice. Theologians stress this when they insist that the supernaturality of the divine life we are invited to share transcends the entire sphere or realm of the natural. But according to St. Anselm, it is the will's affection for justice that enables it to accept this free and gratuitous gift on the part of the Trinity and, already in this life, to love God even more than oneself, and to love him for his own sake and not simply as our good or beatitude. That is why many theologians thought that one could love God in this altruistic unselfish way only with the aid of divine grace or supernatural charity.

The affection for justice as the will's native freedom.

Scotus, however, felt this affection for justice to be something more than an extrinsic gift, added on as it were to the will's intrinsic nature. Even sinners who lack this gratuitous grace or the infused virtue of charity, often perform heroic acts, even laying down their lives or surrendering their own happiness out of love for another individual or person. Even when our will follows its inclination or affection for the advantageous, our intellect often recognizes that we are choosing the less noble and courageous course of action. And in our better moments at least, we admire those who have the strength of will to follow what right reason dictates as best. Scotus argued, in short, that this affection for justice already exists in the very nature of the will. What is more, the inclination to love things objectively in terms of what is just and is due to them moderates the other inclination to seek only the advantageous or one's own happiness above all else. Thus it has a certain liberating effect that frees us to love what is good as it deserves to be loved. Since it has this result, Scotus refers to the affection for justice as the will's congenital or *native freedom*. Indeed, he considers this to be what specifically makes the will not just an intellectual or rational, but a free appetite. Indeed, in one of his latest works, his Paris lectures (II, 6, 2), he referred to this inclination or affection for justice as the will's specific difference or defining characteristic.

Scotus admits the supernatural character of the gratuitous face-to-face vision of God in the afterlife. He argues that if it is not to do violence or destroy our nature as human beings, but rather perfect it in a wonderful and unexpected fashion, there must be built into our nature a natural capacity to receive such a gift. And he sees this as rooted in the natural desire of the intellect to know whatever is knowable and even more in the inclination of the will to love whatever is good—and by reason of its affection for justice, to love each good as it deserves to be loved, namely, for its own sake or intrinsic value.

If we have a natural capacity to receive what is supernatural, you may ask, in what sense can we call what we receive "supernatural"? Scotus gives this explanation. As a free gift on the part of God, it depends exclusively on an action of the divine will itself rather than on any action creatures have the natural ability to perform. And yet, in terms of Aristotle's metaphorical use of "desire," it was a common philosophical axiom in his day to say that every nature, be it animate or inanimate, "desires what perfects it." Consequently Scotus can claim that in virtue of its affection for justice, our will, like our intellect in regard to the beatific vision, has, paradoxically, a *natural desire for the supernatural*. This "desire," however, is not something we are conscious of, but know from divine revelation as to our actual destiny. It is clear then, that Bl. John did not envision the actual order of God's creation as did some later theologians as being a two-storied universe. The lower being what one could call man's natural perfection, the second, his supernatural perfection. For God never intended that we should have a purely natural goal, though this could have been one of the many options he might have selected had he willed a creation other than the one he had graciously chosen.

Anselm's Gedankenexperiment

Scotus recognized that Anselm had introduced his positive notion of the will's freedom (to preserve its rectitude for the sake of that rectitude) as well as his conception of the will's affection for justice, in the context of a discussion of how Lucifer fell from grace (i.e., from a supernatural state that transcended nature) to a state of sin by a willful inordinate love of self, prompted by the will's inclination for the advantageous. Hence Bl. John acknowledged that the Anselmian distinction he was promoting may have originated in the saint's discussion of justice as a supernatural virtue. Yet John insisted he was only developing what was latent in this original conception of the will, and thus doing no injustice to Anselm's basic notion of the nature of free will. For if the will was only an intellective appetite, it might be subject to error or mistakes, but could it ever be free to sin?

He calls attention to Anselm's interesting "thought-experiment" as to what the consequences of such a conception of the will would be. Scientists, we know, often conduct such a *Gedankenexperiment* as Einstein called it, to exclude inappropriate theories that are refuted by experience or empirical data. Anselm selected the angelic nature as the subject of his "experiment," since the consequences of the action-theory he sought to refute stand out more sharply here than they do in the case of a rational animal, as Aristotelians were wont to define a human being. For the drive for self-actualization in a purely spiritual being concerns only the good of the individual rather than the welfare of the species or the race. Scotus describes this medieval bit of science-fiction as follows:

> If one were to think, according to the fictitious situation Anselm postulates in *The Fall of the Devil*, that there was an angel with an affection for the beneficial, but without an affection for justice (i.e., one that had a purely intellectual appetite as such and not one that was free), such an angel would be unable not to will what is beneficial, and unable not to covet such above all. But this would not be imputed to it as sin. For this appetite would be related to intellect as the visual appetite is now related to sight. It would be compelled to follow what is shown to it by the intellect, and being inclined to seek the very best revealed by such a power, for the appetite has nothing to restrain it.
>
> Therefore, [in our will] this affection for justice . . . is the first checkrein on the will's affection for the beneficial. We need not actually

seek that towards which the affection for the benficial inclines us, nor must we seek it above all else. . . This affection for what is just, I say, is the liberty innate to the will, since it represents the first checkrein on this affection for the advantageous. (*Ordinatio* II, 6, 2)

Not only in the angel but in the case of creatures like ourselves, this affection for justice frees our will from the need to always seek itself or the good of the species. It enables a person to evaluate what is good objectively, and according to right reason. It tempers and moderates our affection for the advantageous and the need to seek our own happiness above everything else. What is more, it is only because our will has the potential to will in this way that it is *capax Dei* as theologians put it. That is, capable of sharing the inner love the divine persons have for the divine Godhead.

Two medieval theories of love

This conception of the will enabled Scotus to steer a middle course between two competing theories of love proposed by medieval thinkers in the thirteenth century. Pierre Rousselot describes them in his classic study, *Pour l'Histoire du Problème de l'Amour au Moyen Age*. One he calls the "physical theory" proposed by the Greek philosophers, notably Aristotle and Plato. The other the "ecstatic theory" exemplified in the writings of Christian saints and mystics.

"Physis" is the Greek term for "nature" and the physical theory of love in brief declares that all natural activity is sparked by the drive for self-perfection or self-actualization. Since whatever perfects a thing is its good, we can call all physical activity a form of love. All striving, all endeavor in the universe is nothing else but the imperfect reaching out to perfect itself. The eye loves to see because seeing is the perfection of the eye. The ear to hear because hearing is the perfection of the ear. The nose loves to run, not because a running nose is a perfection, but it does get rid of irritation and infection. And so goes the theory. Biologically speaking, all organic activity is a life-form seeking to keep what it has and to get what it does not have but requires for its existence. When the body needs nourishment, hunger sets up a train of reactions that leads to the search for food. Even the perpetuation of the race through reproduction is a kind of self-extension in which the individual seeks immortality in posterity. As Plato stated it poetically in the *Symposium*, his dialogue on the nature of love, "Penury or poverty is the mother of all love!" Aristotle, his most famous pupil, pointed to other biological examples. Even apparent exceptions like the drone bee's urge for reproduction that leads to his death or the male spider that is eaten by his mate, are explained away as instances of nature seeking to perpetuate itself at the cost of the individual. The latter is of little value compared to that of the species. For, as Cardinale noted above, "pride of place" is given to the universal, and the individual is "relegated to the domain of the accidental and perishable." Even in the case of human behavior the biological analogy obtains. All activity is portrayed in one way or another as a search to fill a need, a want, an emptiness in oneself. The mind hungers for information; the emotions for fulfilment, the lonely for companionship. All action in one way or another is a drive for self-actualization.

We see how this physical theory when applied to the will describes well Bl. John's conception of how this faculty behaves when it chooses to follow its inclination for the advantageous. But for a Christian like himself, this cannot be the whole story. When Greek thought invaded the medieval university campus, this physical theory of love created a dual difficulty for the professional theologian. How, to begin with, can one maintain with St. John that "God is love?" Secondly, how can we fulfil the divine commandment to love God with our whole heart, mind and soul (Mk 12: 30; Lk 10: 27)?

One answer was the "ecstatic theory" of love, exemplified in Christian saints and mystics, who, mindful of St. Paul's warning to his Greek converts in Corinth, realized that Christian charity "is not self-seeking." It is more difficult to define than the physical theory, for ecstatic love seems to require, in part at least, God's gratuitous grace and the supernatural virtue of charity, at least as described by spiritual writers of the Middle Ages. In many respects, they see ecstatic love as the polar opposite of that described by the physical theory. It is altruistic, not egotistic. It puts self in the service of others. It asks: What can I do for *you?* Not, what can I do you *for?* Rather than seeking self-fulfilment, it tends to empty, even to do violence to self, in order to serve Christ in others and to alleviate another's need. Rather than searching for happiness or self-contentment, it discovers it in making another glad. It finds spiritual satisfaction in spending self for those in need, because it sees Christ in the most indigent of his brethren (Mt 25:35-45). And where God himself is concerned, ecstatic love is completely forgetful of self. And in the mystical experience described by saints, there is the desire to be totally absorbed in union with God.

As Rousselot points out, ecstatic love has an element of irrationality and even violence about it—irrationality, for it outruns human reckoning, and in its emotional exhilaration it never counts the cost to self; violence, for the saints, like St. Paul (in Romans 7), see "in their body's members another law at war with the law of the mind." Rather than pampering human nature, they mortify it, for they regard it as "weak flesh, sold into the slavery of sin," always ready, in Paul's words, to "do not the good I will to do, but the evil I do not intend." And like him they ask: "Who can free me from this body under the power of death?'' It is the love of Christ, a love—the saints assure us—that is "stern as death" (Song of Songs 8:6). Commenting on that text, St. Augustine explains: "Since this love slays what we have been, that we may be what we were not; love creates a sort of death in us" (*On the Psalms*, Ps 122). Paul died this death for he said, "The world has been crucified to me, and I to the world" (Gal 6:14). "After all you have died!"—he reminded the Colossians (3:3)—"Your life is hidden now with Christ in God."

In this extreme form, ecstatic love seems more characteristic of the heroic virtue practiced by saints well advanced in spirituality, or who, living as religious, are not bound by family ties and the everyday concerns of ordinary persons living in the world. But even for these secular individuals, where good will prevails, there is not only a need, but an ability to practice something of this love that takes one out of self. Though the cares of this world in which we live today can make this difficult at times, we still recognize the importance to mental health of not letting ourselves be pressured into making our personal problems our sole concern. And there is a special therapeutic feature about self-forgetfulness, as psychologists continually point out to patients who have fallen victim to the epidemic of extreme egotism. And as Scotus assures us, we have the ability to achieve a proper balance if we make proper use of our will, reinforcing by virtuous action its natural inclination or affection for justice.

Scotus' intermediate conception of love.

Scotus' conception of the twofold inclination of our will, it seems, does justice to what is good about both theories of love as well as correcting what is missing or defective about each. On the one hand, the affection for justice explains how we can fulfill the first and greatest of the Christian commandments, to love the Lord our God with our whole heart, whole mind and whole soul, as well as the second—to love our neighbor as ourselves. It thus provides a reasonable alternative to exaggerated versions of the ecstatic theory that it is neither irrational nor does it do violence to nature. For the will's affection for justice only moderates its affection for the advantageous, it does not eliminate it or do violence to it. For guided by right reason, it recognizes we do not serve justice by ignoring our real needs. Is not God himself the author of our human appetites and the desires rooted in our nature? We cannot love all things solely because they are good in themselves; we are constrained by our very humanity to seek also what is good for us. At times even, because of the complexity of human nature, we may find ourselves torn between the love that is self-seeking and the love that is self-giving. But the problem does not lie so much with the will as to recognizing that we are born into this life as infants totally dependent on the care of parents. This is the creature in us, and it is indeed governed largely if not exclusively by one's inclinations for what is advantageous. But we are not meant to remain infants, rather gradually to outgrow this exclusive self-centeredness as we mature and come to recognize that we can never find fulfilment alone but only in giving and sharing what we have with others. This is the divine element in us, the mark of the Trinity in whose likeness we were created. When we seek ourselves, then, it is the creature in us; if at times we forget ourselves, go out of ourselves to give or share what we have, it is the divine in us—the spark of love that is not desire but friendship—the perfect form of love.

As Scotus viewed our human condition, God planned that these two loves be integrated as he believed they were in the state of original innocence. They can again function harmoniously in the ideal family atmosphere where all members are concerned as much with the needs of the others as their own. And when the adolescent leaves the family circle to take his or her place in the adult world, this concern for others should continue to grow. Normally it begins when a young man and a young woman realize they cannot be happy alone, and marry to begin a family of their own. As their family grows, they too become more community minded, concerned with making society a better place for their children than perhaps was their own lot. Marriage has been described as a school of unselfishness, and in God's plan it was meant to begin that process of communual giving that ultimately will prepare them—when the present life is over—to share what God destined them for in giving them existence.

Affection for justice as applied to God

Since this concept of the will as the locus of an affection for justice involves no imperfection in its formal concept, Scotus feels free to attribute it to God as a pure perfection. As such it explains God's love for his infinitely lovable nature, for not to love such would be to do it an injustice. In God there is no real distinction between the divine will, its inclination or affection for justice, and the act of love that proceeds from the divine will in regard to the divine essence. For, as Scotus put in his philosophical prayer to God, "You are the ultimate in simplicity, having no really distinct parts, or no realities in your essence which are not really the same." Consequently, God would not be God if this love for the divine nature and the concomitant happiness it brings were not there. Hence, God's love for his goodness seems to be a necessary act, an integral part of the divine nature. As Scotus worded it in his prayer:

You are happy, indeed you are by nature, happiness itself, because you are in possession of yourself. You are the clear vision of yourself and the most joyful love, and although you are self-sufficient and happy in yourself alone, you still understand in a single act everything that can be known. At one and the same time you possess the power to freely and contingently will each thing that can be caused, and by willing it through your volition, cause it to be. Most truly then you are of infinite power.

Despite this necessity in the divine will, Scotus claims there must be still something basically free about any love that stems from the will. As Bl. John views it in the case of the divine will at least, necessity is not incompatible with freedom. Clearly love for his own goodness seems to be a necessary attribute of divinity, yet that same will from which this love proceeds, is unquestionably free, at least to create or not create. Scotus felt that if one understands the affection for justice as it exists in its full perfection in God, it would explain to some extent, the paradox of God's freedom and necessity about what he loves. God's goodness is infinite and the inclination to love such goodness is infinitely demanding; but the goodness characteristic of any creature is finite, and as such can exercise no compelling or necessitating force on God's creative will. Therefore whatever his creative love brings into existence will always have a contingent character about it. But even in its love for the divine nature, God's will is free according to St. Anselm's positive definition of free will, for it loves that nature for its own sake, and as Scotus explains, "as other," that is to say, as something not loved privately or jealously as an egotist might love it, but as something to be loved by others. Scotus also explains that we regard lack of firmness in a will in doing what right reason dictates to be an imperfection in ourselves. Firmness of will by contrast, therefore, must be a perfection and perfectly compatible with freedom. It is under this aspect that Scotus explains the fact that there is an inevitablity with its concomitant necessity about God's love for his own goodness.

But where creatures, whose goodness is finite, are concerned, God is free, as we said, to create as he chooses. Does this mean that God is wholly free to deal with creation in an arbitrary and whimsical fashion? Does not his affection for justice impel him in some way to give to his creatures what they need, or from our viewpoint, to provide them with what seems to be their due? Theologians, like Aquinas, when they treat of divine justice ascribe a two-fold justice to God, one he owes to himself, and that which he owes to creatures. With his usual subtlety Scotus questions this twofold conception of God's justice (*Ordinatio* IV, 46). What God gives to creatures will always be a free gift, not something he is compelled in any way by his nature to grant to them. There is but one justice in God, Bl. John insists, that which he owes to his own goodness. But that goodness is infinite, and what he owes to it is not justice to creatures but rather liberality since he has freely chosen to create them. This liberality, however, goes beyond anything strict justice would demand, for it over-rewards the good and is merciful to the sinner. But where persons are concerned, we impute this liberality to him as a kind of secondary justice. From a more profound viewpoint, however, it is rather part and parcel of what God owes to his own divine goodness. In his prayer, cited above, Scotus expressed this conviction when he wrote: "Communicating the rays of your goodness most liberally, you are boundless good to whom as the most lovable thing of all every single being in its own way comes back to you as its ultimate end."

How creation comes back to God as its ultimate end

When we add this notion of justice and liberality to our interpretation of God's purpose in creation we can understand better why Scotus gave the following description of how God's love extends to the whole of creation. For if the Trinity of divine persons love the divine nature they share in common in an objective way as a beloved object, then they would want it to be loved by individual co-lovers distinct in nature from their own, since their infinite nature could not be replicated. This is how Scotus views the motive for creation as an integral constituent of a single act of love—single from the standpoint that there is but one act of love in God, but multiple in terms of the objects and the way it tends towards those objects. It is in this vein he describes how in an orderly fashion the divine will tends towards the various objects of its love.

> Everyone who wills in a reasonable way, first wills the end and secondly that which immediately attains the end, and thirdly other things that are more remotely ordered to the attainment of his end. And so it is that God, who is most reasonable, . . . first wills the end, and in this his act is perfect, and his intellect is perfect, and his will is happy. Secondly, he wills those things which are immediately ordered to him, . . . namely, the elect who attain him immediately, and this as it were reflexively, willing others to love with him the very object of his love. . . Hence he first loves himself ordinately and consequently not inordinately in an envious or jealous manner. Secondly, he wills to have other co-lovers, and this is nothing other than willing that others have his love in themselves. . . Thirdly, however, he wills them to have those things which are necessary to attain his end, namely, the gift of grace. Fourthly, he wills for their sake things that are more remote—for instance this sensible world—in order that it may serve them. . . . Hence, man will be the raison d'être of the sensible world, whether it be because God wills the sensible world to be ordered to predestined man or whether it be because his more immediate concern is not that the sensible world exist, but rather that [through it] man love him. (*Ordinatio* III, [suppl.] d. 33)

CHRISTOLOGY

Of all created individuals capable of loving God's divine nature in this objective way, of loving "with him the very object of his love," Christ's soul stands out as the most important of all such created "co-lovers." And that leads Scotus to give a special interpretation to the motive of the Incarnation. He writes

> I say that the incarnation of Christ was not foreseen as occasioned [by sin], but was immediately foreseen from all eternity by God as a good closer to the end [that God had in mind in creating]. Thus Christ in his human nature is foreseen as nearer to that end than the others—speaking of those who were to be given grace and glory. (*Ordinatio* III , d. 19)

This marks a turning point in the theological literature on the motive of the Incarnation, and precisely how redemption relates to the humanity of Jesus. Unlike many of his predecessors, Scotus was not primarily concerned with what God might have done in another order, for instance, if Adam had not sinned, although he will have something to say about this as well. But it is important to keep in mind that he began with the actual order—with the fact of the Incarnation as it actually occurred in all its details. And thus Scotus also takes into account that the complete motive for Christ's Incarnation includes also the prevision of Adam's fall and his subsequent redemption. For he remembered only too well how Peter Lombard, the author of their theological textbook, began his treatment of "Christology" in Book III of his *Sentences* with that quotation from St. Paul to the Galatians (4:4-5): "When the fulness of time was come, God sent forth his Son made of a woman, made under the law, to redeem them that were under the law, that we might receive the adoption of sons."

Humanity of Christ—Creation's "Firstborn"

But "as a good more proximate to the end" in what order would these various aspects of the Son's Incarnation be wanted by a divine will with an affection for justice? What was primarily intended? secondarily? and so on. To begin with, was it primarily the human nature in Christ God wanted as co-lover? And since no human being could share the inner love life of the Trinity without glory, and glory in the next life without merits in this, and without grace no merits, how were all these intended by an infinitely orderly will guided by infinite wisdom? This was the question Bl. John asked himself.

Where persons were concerned, we said above, God wanted individuals to be part of the order of the universe, before he wanted the sort of natures that would give each a special role to play. And where individual subjects through the misuse of that nature, freely willed, would fall from grace, but through God's infinite liberality would be restored to the kingdom of God, they could again freely choose to so love God as to merit eventual glory. How were all these facets of our human condition interrelated? And how did Christ figure in? he whom St. Paul tells us in his letter to the Colossians (1:15-18) was "the image of the invisible God, the first-born of all creatures; in him everything in heaven and on earth was created, things visible and invisible, whether thrones or dominations, principalities or powers; all were created through him, and for him; he is before all else that is. In him everything continues in being." (cf also Eph 1:9-10). How did a particular divine person, not just divinity, become hypostatically involved in creation? For "he" in the Pauline text refers not to a human person, but to the Son of God himself. For God so loved the world, the Gospel tells us (Jn 3: 16), that he sent his only beloved Son into it that whoever freely believes in him might not die, but have eternal life. How then would God in his mercy choose to redeem humanity? In the most economical way possible or in the extravagant way of an ecstatic lover?

God, a most orderly lover

A seemingly impossible task to sort this all out, but that is what Scotus tried to do when, as a bachelor theologian, he had to spell out what he believed of Christ. For he was convinced that God in his infinite goodness, knowledge, and love, was a "most orderly lover." And though he loved with but a single act of love, directed primarily to his own goodness, that act of voluntary love spilled over to communicate something of his own goodness to creation. But this is not something he was compelled to do, for no finite good can compel an infinite will, but such creates freely, as an artist does, who is free to produce what he chooses. When God does produce, however, what he creates must do justice to his art. It is this complexity of the one divine will-act and the diverse ways it affects both the divine goodness it wills firmly as well as the secondary objects that represent its free communication of that goodness to creatures—it is this complexity in the will-act, I say, that theologians wish to distinguish conceptually. Scotus, we recall, insisted that only to his own goodness is God strictly a debtor, loving it as is its due, firmly and therefore necessarily. "But where creatures are concerned he is debtor rather to his generosity, in the sense that he gives creatures what their nature demands, which exigency in them is set down as something just, a kind of secondary object of this justice as it were." (*Ordinatio* IV, d. 46)

It is the order that runs through this complexity Scotus sees in creation that he tried to sketch in some detail in his Christology. It is in this sense that he sought to solve the theological question as to what motivated the Incarnation, in all its complexity.

Glorification of Christ's human nature

To begin with, how did the hypostatic union fit in with God's plan? Specifically, why divinize this human nature that the trinity of divine persons wanted as a created co-lover? Scotus tells us in explaining Christ's predestination. (*Ordinatio* III , d. 7, q. 3)

> Predestination consists in preordaining someone first of all to glory and then to other things which are ordered to glory. Now the human nature in Christ was predestined to be glorified, and in order to be glorified, it was predestined to be united to the Word, inasmuch as such glory as it was granted would never have been conferred on this nature had it not been so united. Now if it would not be fitting to ordain one to such glory if certain merits were absent, whereas it would be fitting if they were present, then such merits are included in the predestination. And so it would seem that this union by way of fitness is ordered to this glory, although it is not exactly as merit that it falls under this predestination. And just as it is foreordained that this nature be united to the Word, so it is predestined that the Word be man and that this man be the Word.

What he tells us here is that glory (which refers to the human condition in the afterlife, the beatific sharing in the inner life of the divine persons) of Jesus' human nature is what God first intended. This union with God, we said earlier, is something that transcends anything demanded by human nature and is a pure gift on the part of God. In this life, grace—with the indwelling of the Trinity it brings to the soul—is an anticipation of glory. "Now we see through a glass darkly," Paul tells us, "but then face to face."(1 Cor 13:12) When faith becomes vision, grace becomes glory. Howsoever we conceive of this grace/glory in the soul, whether as a habit as the Scholastics with their Aristotelian background did, or as an intimate union or relationship with God, it admits of degrees. As Paul put it, just as star differs from star in brightness, so will resurrected humanity differ from one individual to another in glory (1 Cor 15:41-42). According to Scotus, the degree of glory in individuals other than Christ, though properly speaking a gratuitous gift, God conditions on their free cooperation, and in proportion to their response, accepting action on their part as "meritorius." In this sense, "merit" in the case of beatified also falls under God's predestination of the elect. In the case of Christ, as the "firstborn of many brethren," grace/glory existed in the highest possible degree, according to Scotus. This could not be strictly merited, but it was fitting that such grace and glory be given to that created nature that the Word had assumed personally. Hence, this hypostatic union which functioned in the place of personal merit, also fell under the predestination of Christ's humanity to glory.

Reason for the hypostatic union

But this raised a doubt in Bl. John's mind. If God was a most orderly lover, which of these two aspects of Christ's Incarnation would he want most of all? As Scotus words the question: "Which did God intend first, the union of this nature with the Word, or its ordination to glory?" He suggests this answer:

> Now the sequence in which the creative artist evolves his plan is the very opposite of the way he puts it into execution. One can say, however, that in the order of execution God's union with a human nature is naturally prior to his granting it the greatest grace and glory. We could presume, then, that it was in the reverse order that he intended them, so that God would first intend that some nature, not the highest, should receive the highest glory, proving thereby he was not constrained to grant glory in the same measure as he bestowed natural perfection. Then secondly, as it were, he willed that this nature should subsist in the Person of the Word, so that the angel might not be subject to a [mere] man.

Since we tend to think of God as inviting created persons to share the divine life, and such is ordinarily the case, Scotus anticipates this challenge to his interpretation of what occurred in the Incarnation.

> But you may object that primarily predestination regards the person and hence one must first find some person to whom God predestined (1) the glory and then (2) this union with reference to the glory. Now you will find no divine Person to whom God predestined this union [as a means of glory]. Obviously he did not do so to the Word insofar as he is the Word. Neither was this union predestined as a means of glory to the Word as subsisting in a human nature, because to the extent that he subsists in this way, the union is already included.
>
> I reply: we can deny that predestination concerns persons only, for if God can love a good other than himself, not only when it is a person, but also when it is a nature, then for its sake he can also select and ordain in advance some good suitable to it. Consequently, he can choose (1) glory and (2) the union as a means of glory, not only for the person, but also for some nature. It is true, however, that in all cases other than this, predestination does concern the person, for in no other instance has God foreordained a good to a [human] nature without by that very fact foreordaining it also to some person, for the simple reason that no other human nature subsists save in a created person to whom the good can be foreordained. But in our case this is not so.

Was the Incarnation required for redemption?

It is in this connection that he challenges the interpretation that the Incarnation was primarily oriented to redemption. "Many authorities," he admits, "seem to say as much when they declare the Son of God would never have become incarnate had man not fallen." Even the liturgist who composed the Easter "Exultet" seemed to be suggesting that we should be thankful for Adam's sin that had brought us so great a redeemer. Scotus had his own way of interpreting this "felix culpa" as something God permitted as it gave his "firstborn" an occasion to show how important it was to him, and to what lengths his love for these "adopted siblings" (Gal 4:5) would go, lest he lose any of those given him by his Father, for "these you have given me, they are really yours" (Jn 17:9).

Some theologians had suggested that certain creatures were created only because God foresaw that others would sin, and they were destined or predestined as replacements, as it were. Scotus wanted no part of this opinion; for, he argued, in such a case one individual would have reason to rejoice in another's downfall, and no one should be thankful that another has sinned. He refers to his earlier discussion (*Ordinatio* I, d. 41) where he argued that "the predestination of anyone to glory is prior by nature to the prevision of sin or the damnation of anyone." If this is true of the elect in general, then:

> So much the more then is this true of the predestination of that soul which was destined beforehand to possess the very highest glory possible. For it seems to be universally true that one who wills ordinately, and not inordinately, first intends what is nearer the end; and just as he first intends one to have glory before grace, so among those to whom he has foreordained glory, he who wills ordinately, would seem to intend first the glory of the one he wishes to be nearest the end, and therefore he intends glory to this soul [of Christ] before he wills glory to any other soul, and to every other soul he wills glory before taking into account the opposite of these habits [namely, the sin or damnation of anyone].
>
> Authorities to the contrary can all be explained in the sense that Christ would not have come as redeemer, if man had not sinned. Perhaps, too, he would not have been able to suffer, since there would have been no need of a union with a passible body for this soul glorified from its first moment of existence, to which God chose to give not only the highest glory but also willed that it be always present. If man had not sinned, of course, there would have been no need of a redemption. Still it does not seem to be solely because of the redemption that God predestined this soul to such glory, since the redemption or the glory of the souls to be redeemed is not comparable to the glory of the soul of Christ. Neither is it likely that the highest good in the whole of creation is something that merely chanced to take place, and that only because of some lesser good. Nor is it probable that God predestined Adam to such a good before he predestined Christ. Yet all this would follow, yes, and even something more absurd. If the predestination of Christ's soul was for the sole purpose of redeeming others, it would follow that in foreordaining Adam to glory God would have had to foresee him as having fallen into sin before he could have

predestined Christ to glory. Consequently, we can say that God selected for his heavenly choir all the angels and men he wished to have with their varied degrees of perfection, and all this before considering either the sin or the punishment of the sinner. No one therefore is predestined simply because God foresaw another would fall, lest anyone have reason to rejoice at the misfortune of another.

One of the reasons for assuming that redemption might be the main purpose of the Incarnation was that only a God-man could atone for sin. Scotus questioned the validity of the argument on which such a claim was originally made, namely, that since sin was an offense against an infinite being, it could only be compensated for by a redemptive act by a divine person. His objection was that this mistakenly attributes an action of infinite value to a finite creature. No finite agent is capable of such an infinite action, whether that action be good or wicked. God could have given the redemptive role to a created person, by giving such a savior the grace whereby he or she could have performed an act so loving and pleasing to God that it would have offset God's displeasure at the original offense. And, it could have had its repercussions for the whole human race, had God accepted such an act as redemptive. For as Paul put it in his letter to the Romans (5:19): "Just as through one man's disobedience all became sinners, so through one man's obedience all shall become just."

Neither did Scotus believe that Christ's redemptive acts, formally and precisely speaking, were of infinite value. No created act strictly speaking merits grace or glory since the union with the divine that these entail will always be a gratuitous gift on the part of God. But inasmuch as God, in his liberality and mercy, rather than out of any strict obligation in justice, accepts certain actions of a creature already in a state of grace as merit, so too the Trinity accepts the theandric acts of Jesus as of inexhaustible and thus quasi-infinite merit for the human race.

> And just as the Word foresaw the passion of Christ as something to be offered for the predestined and elect, and so efficaciously offered it in fact, so also did the entire Trinity accept his passion efficaciously, and because it was offered efficaciously for none without being accepted from all eternity, therefore [Christ] has merited for them the first grace leading eventualy to glory. (*Ordinatio* III, d. 19)

Mary, the Mother of God, was the first to profit by Christ's merits, and in a most wonderful and extraordinary way, Scotus believed.

MARIOLOGY

Though Scotus did not explicitly apply his theory of the predestination of Christ to Mary his mother, the later Scotists often did so, especially in their defense of her Immaculate Conception, inspired by Bl. John's own striking defense of this prerogative, both at Oxford and later at Paris. And they had every reason to do so, for it does follow implicitly from what he said of the primacy of Christ and of his merits. Indeed, the very text from Romans (1:3-4) he chose to introduce his question about the predestination of Christ, implicitly recognized that as "a descendant of David according to the flesh," the Son of God had a human mother. And according to what was said above, about the elect predestined to glory, she too would have been so predestined from all eternity, and the pre-redeeming grace she owed to Christ's merits would have been her "first grace leading eventually to glory." Yet at the time Scotus presented his arguments for his belief in Mary's Immaculate Conception, it was little more than a theological opinion, and to present it otherwise would have been unprofessional and brash.

It may be difficult for those of us who are not professional theologians, or historians of theology, to realize how slowly some of the important truths came to be clarified and eventually accepted by the Magisterium of the Church as divinely revealed. Mary's Immaculate Conception is one of those truths. Some of the great theologians and doctors of the Church could not accept it, including such saints as Bernard of Clairvaux, Thomas Aquinas, and even Bonaventure. Even Scotus' courageous defense of it, carefully nuanced in its respect for the authority of Scripture and the Church, as it was, aroused animosity, as we noted in speaking of his Paris regency in Part II. If we digress for a bit on the historical background of this controversy, it may help us better to appreciate the important contribution Bl. John made in academic circles to reverse the theological opposition to a prerogative of Mary he had been taught to love before coming to Paris.

The story of how Mary's Immaculate Conception came to be explicitly recognized and eventually defined by Pius IX in the "Ineffabilis Deus" as a dogma of faith has long interested theologians. It illustrates how complex the working of the Holy Spirit is in the Church in bringing to light the full content of divine revelation. It involves not only the disputations of theologians but the role played by the *sensus fidelium* or the living faith of the common Christian.

Feast of Mary's Conception

In this case that living faith centered on a feast to honor St. Ann's conception of Mary. If John the Baptist was cleansed of original sin in Elizabeth's womb, what of Mary who would be even more intimately connected with the redeemer? The apocryphal *Gospel of the Birth of Mary* and the *Protoevangelium* already drew parallels between the angelic appearances to Joachim and his wife and those recounted of Zachary in Luke's Gospel. A feast embodying these popular beliefs originated in the East. Though it began as a Feast of St. Ann, the emphasis even then was on the exceptional holiness of the child she would bear, a child who would be sanctified already in the womb like Jeremiah and John the Baptist.

Only when it was introduced in the West as the Feast of Mary's Conception did it provoke the opposition that led to a significant development of Mariology. Before the Norman invasion the feast had become popular with the Saxons, but after 1066 it underwent a period of eclipse. William the Conqueror conferred many of the episcopal sees and abbacies in England upon his ecclesiastical followers. The general contempt of these newcomers for Anglo-Saxon customs, and the fact that the feast seemed based on apocryphal works, may have been the reason why it was suppressed in many dioceses. Saxon pride, however, kept the feast alive, and reputed miracles helped it to regain its popularity. One such was the widely circulated story of Mary's appearance to Helsin, the Abbot of Ramsey, whom she had saved from shipwreck and authorized to celebrate her conception on the 8th of December. In 1129 the Council of London confirmed the feast for the whole English province. From there it spread naturally enough to Normandy and other parts of Europe. Though miraculous confirmations accounted for this popular appeal, it was the Benedictine monk, Eadmer of Canterbury (d. 1124), who provided his countrymen with a sound theological argument for celebrating Mary's conception itself. If Jeremiah and John the Baptist were sanctified before birth, how much more should Mary as the Queen of Angels and the tabernacle of the Son of God be completely untouched by sin. This idea that, as sanctified in the womb, Mary may never have contracted original sin, was expressed as early as the ninth century. But it had been lost sight of until rediscovered by Eadmer. Since he was the secretary, disciple and biographer of the Archbishop and Primate of England, it is not surprising that his unsigned treatise as late as the 14th century was mistakenly attributed to St. Anselm of Canterbury himself.

St. Bernard of Clairvaux

If Eadmer's interpretation overcame one theological objection to the feast, it created a far more serious one. For as early as the sixth century, theologians had accepted the theory that original sin was transmitted to Adam's progeny by sexual intercourse. It claimed sin was contracted the moment a newly created soul was infused into a seminally conceived fetus. Only because concupiscence played no part in Mary's virginal conception of Christ was his human soul immaculate. How then could Ann's conception of Mary itself be holy, or sin absent, where libido was present? asked

St. Bernard in his passionate letter to the Canons of Lyons. He chided them for spoiling their splendid record in liturgical matters by introducing this novel feast which, as he put it, the Church ignores, which reason disavows, and tradition disapproves. "Are we more learned or pious than the Fathers?" And are we really honoring the Mother of God when we attribute to Ann what is unique to Mary, her immaculate conception of a child? "Where would her singular prerogative be, if we attribute this same privilege to her mother? This is not honoring Mary but detracting from her honor." For a century and a half this argument of Bernard was repeated. It was one that Scotus had to answer in his defense of Mary's prerogative, for he saw no way to gainsay or reinterpret the mind of the saint. He could only point out where Bernard's thinking had gone wrong. The term "conception"—John Duns insisted—has more than one meaning. It may refer either to the "mixing of seeds" when the fetus is formed, or to the instant when the organized embryo becomes a human being. There was no libido present when a month or more after Joachim's marital embrace, the developing fetus in Ann received Mary's newly created and pre-sanctified soul.

St. Thomas Aquinas

Far more serious was the objection voiced by St. Thomas Aquinas:

> If the soul of the Blessed Virgin had never incurred the stain of original sin, this would be derogatory to the dignity of Christ, by reason of his being the universal savior of all. Consequently after Christ, who as the universal savior of all, needed not to be saved, the purity of the Blessed Virgin holds the highest place. For Christ did not contract original sin in any way whatever, but was holy in his very conception, according to Luke 1:35: 'The Holy which shall be born of thee, shall be called the Son of God.' But the Blessed Virgin did indeed contract original sin, but was cleansed therefrom before her birth from the womb." (*Summa theologica.* III, 27, 2, ad 2)

This, as Scotus saw it, was really the crucial difficulty he had to address before serious contemporary theologians, of the same persuasion as Bonaventure and Aquinas before them, could accept the Immaculate Conception even as a possibility.

As for those who cited the widespread celebration of the feast of Mary's Conception, even though the Holy See had not sanctioned it, Aquinas already had this answer.

> Although the Church of Rome does not celebrate the Conception of the Virgin, yet it tolerates the custom of certain churches that do keep that

feast; wherefore this is not to be entirely reprobated. Nevertheless the celebration of this feast does not give us to understand that she was holy in her conception. But since it is not known when she was sanctified, the feast of her Sanctification rather than the feast of her Conception is kept on the day of her conception." (Ibid, ad 3)

But Scotus remembered the exciting day, when shortly after his ordination, he sat at the feet of William of Ware, the first Oxford Franciscan to defend the opinion that Mary may not have contracted orginal sin. But even if he had erred in overpraising Mary, and she had been stained by Adam's fall, William pointed out that there was still another acceptable way to celebrate the conception itself, not just Mary's sanctification. For it was from Mary's flesh that Christ's own body would be formed. Even at the end of the thirteenth century, it was clear that the immaculist sense was far from being the usual interpretation of the Mary's feast on December 8th, and this more than anything helped to spread its celebration, especially at Paris where the precise object and rationale of the Feast of the Conception remained a controversial issue well into the 14th century. Even in England it was not until two decades after Scotus' death that the provincial council of Canterbury decided to celebrate the feast in the sense proposed by Eadmer or pseudo-Anselm.

Henry of Ghent's Public Disputation

During Scotus' student days at Oxford, the deteriorating political situation between France and England caused Philip the Fair to issue his edict of 1293 expelling all the Scots and English from France. The students returning to Oxford from the French capital told of the solemn public debate the preceding year between the two most prominent secular masters of theology at the University of Paris, Henry of Ghent and Godfrey of Fontaines. Both admitted the common opinion that Mary contracted original sin, but as St. Thomas had indicated earlier no one knew the precise moment after animation that her soul was sanctified. It was during Advent, around December 8th, that Henry of Ghent was conducting his fifteenth quodlibetal disputation where anyone in the audience could raise a question. Because of the proximity of the feast, some student, probably from England, asked the master a particularly controversial question: "Is the conception of the Virgin Mary to be celebrated precisely *by reason of her conception*?" The student theologian knew many back home believed Mary had never contracted original sin. They claimed the Archbishop of Canterbury and Primate of England himself supported this view, because they credited St. Anselm with the authorship of Eadmer's unsigned tract. But here in Paris, as Bonaventure had noted, no master had ever accepted such a theory. Henry knew well enough the tricky question he was being asked to field. Was Mary's feast really a celebration of her conception, rather than her sanctification? As Alexander of Hales had pointed out half a century earlier, as used by the Paris theologians "sanctification" had a technical meaning. It meant purification of a soul that had contracted original sin, and that is why, Hales explained, Christ's soul was never said to be sanctified. But Mary's was, and the Franciscan masters that succeeded Hales (John of La Rochelle, Odo Rigaux, and William of Melitona) had explicitly asked how and when it took place with reference to the creation and infusion of her soul into flesh that had been tainted in conception. Bonaventure, who succeeded them, knew of the "foreign opinion"—as the Italians at Paris were wont to call the immaculist interpretation that came from the British Isles, for he explained it at length, before—reluctantly perhaps—rejecting it, for no university teacher he had ever heard in his years at Paris had ever defended it. But times were changing, and especially the way the ordinary laity felt about Mary's conception. Henry felt he could satisfy both sides—the piety of the faithful on the one hand by denying there was any appreciable period of time during which Mary's soul remained in a state of sin, and still it was sanctified from the infection of original sin that came from its infusion in the tainted embryo. In one of the longest and most detailed of the fifteen questions fielded during his quodlibet that day, Henry came up with a mind-boggling theory that must have left his listeners astounded.

The Meaning of 'Conception'

He began, innocently enough, by pointing out every liturgical feast is celebrated by reason of a person's sanctity or sanctification. Hence it cannot be the act of conception but the hour, the moment, the time of sanctification that is being celebrated. "Conception," however, could be understood in various ways. There is the conception of the seed (*conceptio seminis*) when fetal life begins. A month or so later, depending on the sex, a rational soul is created and infused in the growing organism. This moment of animation, as all theologians agree, marks the "conception of the human being" (*conceptio hominis*). If this moment of animation marks the "conception as regards the world," Henry explained, then the moment the soul is sanctified may be called a "conception as regards God." Basing his computations on the date of Mary's birthday (September 8), Henry points out that December the 8th, the day the Normans celebrate the feast, must be the "the conception of the bare seed" (*conceptio nudi seminis*). Since there is nothing sacred about this biological event, "conception" in this sense cannot be precisely what is being commemorated. "If they celebrate this day 'by reason of conception,' it must be the other sort of conception they have in mind," namely, the date of animation by the rational soul on January 11th when her soul was created and infused into her body. This moment could also be called her nativity within the womb. But inasmuch as the seminally conceived flesh has this morbid quality (*qualitas morbida*), the soul in contacting it contracts original sin automatically as it were. But once sin is present, sanctification, by definition, becomes possible.

Sanctification

Since sanctification is what is being celebrated, the real question the inquirer who posed it wants answered, is: Does the moment of sanctification coincide with that of animation? If the two moments do not coincide, then there are two possibilities, namely, either (1) once the soul is infused into the body and is infected with sin, it is *immediately sanctified* so that for no continuous period of time does it remain in a state of sin, or else (2) there is a *period of time* in which Mary's soul remained in a state of original sin, whether it be long or short, Henry does not care.

Henry, however, wished to go still further. He believed he could show that the instant of *conception and sanctification coincide for all practical purposes*. For one can distinguish within a single instant of time two distinct aspects of *nature* one of which is prior, the other posterior. According to this *priority of nature* Mary's soul can be first in a state of sin and afterwards in a state of grace. In an extremely long and involved argument, based in part upon Aristotle's physics of motion and change, and partly upon a curious example of how a falling millstone will reverse the direction of a bean thrown against its underside, he attempted to prove this philosophically.

The Bean and the Millstone

From an Aristotelian standpoint, sin and grace represent contrary or opposing forms that cannot coexist in the human soul as their *subject*. On the other hand, according to Aristotle, contrary forms *causally affect one another*. Grace expels the state of sin, and vice versa, since the two cannot simultaneously inform the soul as their subject. But if the presence of grace is what causes the sin to leave, grace must somehow exist if it is to act upon sin. But this means that what acts and what is acted upon must *somehow coexist causally*. To show how this paradoxical situation is possible, Henry appeals to his "Gedankenexperiment" of the bean and the falling millstone. For Aristotle analyzed continuous or rectilinear motion as well as what happens when a moving object recoils or reverses its movement on striking an unyielding barrier. In such a case, says Aristotle, the forward and the reverse movements are opposed and, as discontinuous, they are distinct and radically different from one another. Henry, however, uses his "thought-experiment" to blur this sharp distinction, for to the eye at least the falling millstone seems to continue its downward motion with no interruption whereas that of the bean is reversed when it strikes the millstone. Despite their opposite direction, the last instant of forward motion coincides with the first instant of reverse movement and the reversal of direction takes on the time characteristics of continuous rectilinear motion.

Henry sees this as proof that there is a mid-point between Aristotle's opposites of continuous and discontinuous change. Because of his great devotion to Mary, he sees a way to shrink the interval between her contracting original sin and her subsequent sanctification to an absolute zero time-wise. For at one and the same instant of time, he argues, there can be two distinct "signs of nature." (*Signum* or "sign" was the mathematical designation for a non- dimensional unit, such as a point in time or space. "Signs of nature" was the technical expression philosophers used to distinguish conceptually distinct items that were coincident temporally, but were so interrelated or ordered that one by its nature was prior or presupposed by the other, but not vice versa.) Sanctification, by definition, presupposed the contraction of original sin, but in Mary's case— Henry was saying—they occurred in one and the same instant of time.

In the first sign Mary's soul contracts original sin, but in the other, she is sanctified and continues to remain in that state for her entire life. Since the flow of time is analogous to that of spatial movement, Henry maps his time-distinction on linear co-ordinates. Let the millstone represent the bodily flesh and the bean Mary's spiritual soul; and let the moment the bean touches the millstone represent the instant Mary's soul was created and infused into her body. The downward movement of the bean represents the time Mary's soul was in a state of grace; its upward movement the time her soul fell under the shadow of sin cast by the millstone. Since Mary's soul did not temporally preexist its infusion into her body, however, this dimension shrinks to the initial zero point at which the bean touches the millstone and at once begins to move downward. If there is no rest-interval between the upward motion of the bean and its reversal on striking the millstone, the two contrary movements coincide to the same extent as the last instant of earlier motion overlaps with the first instant of later motion.

Such was Henry's canny solution to a most controversial question. Evidently, it left his divided audience, if they could follow his involved reasoning, both astounded and probably speechless. For it claimed the Feast of the Conception could be so interpreted as to satisfy both parties. For all practical purposes, Mary was never for any span of time, however short its duration, in a state of original sin. Notwithstanding, she did contract it the instant her soul was created and animated her body.

William of Ware

No sooner had Henry proposed this bizarre solution than it was attacked as philosophically nonsensical by Godfrey of Fontaines, the other great secular master of theology of Scotus' student days. Though the King of France had expelled all the British students from his country in 1293, and the following year King Edward I forbade any passage of ships from the British Isles to France, the English students returning from Paris brought word of Henry's astounding solution. William of Ware was the young Franciscan bachelor lecturing that year on the *Sentences* in the Oxford study house. In the appropriate distinction of the third book, he posed the question: "Was the Blessed Virgin conceived in original sin?" There is one opinion, he said, "that says she was conceived in original sin and in the same instant purged and sanctified, but in one 'sign' and in another 'sign' of the same instant." This is a clear reference to Henry, though William does not mention him by name—it was not customary for lecturers to name contemporaries, since their students were expected to know who held such current opinions. As Godfrey of Fontaines will do in Paris, Ware refutes this absurd view of Henry's as a contradiction in terms, for it assumes duality in simultaneity.

There is another opinion, Ware goes on to say, that maintains she did not contract original sin.

> And this I wish to hold, for if I must be wrong, since I am not certain as to the other, I prefer to err by excess in attributing some prerogative to Mary, than to err by defect, diminishing or denying her some prerogative that she does have. . . . Therefore, I wish to show first the possibility; second, the congruity; third, the actuality; fourth, the degree of grace; fifth, that the feast of the conception is to be celebrated in this sense; and sixth, the feast is still to be celebrated, even if she were conceived in original sin.

Among the student priests at the Oxford friary sitting in the straw-strewn floor at Ware's feet that day was John Duns. It was probably the first time in his studies he heard a theologian willing to defend an immaculist interpretation of the Feast of Mary's Conception that was growing in popularity among the commonfolk in England and Normandy. The grounds on which Ware justified its possibility presupposed St. Augustine's theory of how original sin was transmitted. Like Henry of Ghent, William believed that as long as the seminally conceived flesh has this "morbid quality," it would infect the newly created soul when it first animated the embryonic body. But Ware argued that

> The mass of flesh from which the body of the Virgin was formed was simultaneously conceived seminally but cleansed. Insofar as it was of seminal origin it has a morbid quality, but insofar as it was that from which the Virgin's body must be formed, it was cleansed. I do not say it was

sanctified, for only something in which sin and grace subsist, such as the soul, can be sanctified. In other human beings, original sin is contracted when the soul is joined to flesh that has this morbid quality from the parents sowing the seed. Since this infection or morbid quality is not of the substance of flesh, but is really distinct and separable from it, it was possible for God to preserve this mass from infection or morbidity, insofar as the body of the Virgin would be formed from it, although the mass of flesh would have been infected so far as its sowers were concerned.

To indicate how this might have taken place, William cites a remark of St. Augustine that even if Christ's body had not been virginally conceived, his soul would not have contracted original sin if God had cleansed the flesh before creating and infusing the soul.

It was quite possible, therefore, that God could have preserved Mary from contagion of original sin by purifying her body before animating it with a soul. Thus William proves his first point (possibility) from reason. The second (fittingness) and the third (actuality) are proved from authority. For as St. Anselm had pointed out: "Assuredly, it was fitting that the Virgin be beautified with a purity than which a greater cannot be conceived, except for God's (*De conceptu Virginali*, c. 18)." Scotus, too, would use this same quotation in his initial arguments. As proof that God actually did so, Ware could find no explicit text in either Scripture or the early Fathers of the Church. But many had attributed to Mary that verse in the Song of Songs (4:7): "You are all-beautiful, my beloved, and there is no blemish in you." Those Saxons, who sought to justify and spread the celebration of the Feast of Mary's Conception in an immaculist sense, appealed to this text so commonly applied to Mary. The famous Augustinian friar, Alexander Neckham (d. 1217), had explicitly claimed "no blemish" referred to original as well as actual sin, and William quotes him as his first authority, along with less explicit and more general remarks of Richard of St. Victor and Augustine about Mary's lack of sin. He also insisted certain statements of St. Anselm could be interpreted in an immaculist sense.

Evaluation

Had Eadmer's unsigned tract and other works on Mary's conception not been falsely attributed to such a great authority in England as St. Anselm of Canterbury, perhaps William's defense of the Immaculate Conception would have provoked more opposition than it did. Most theologians at least refused to accept his interpretation as anything but a rash opinion, though churchmen were reluctant to oppose it too vigorously, lest they disturb the belief of the common faithful concerning Mary's absolute purity.

Five years of theological study would pass before John would have to present his own lectures on the *Sentences*, as William did. In the third book, distinction three, where Peter Lombard treats of how Christ's body was formed from Mary's flesh, John knew that he too, like William of Ware at Oxford and St. Bonaventure a generation earlier at Paris, would have to deal with the problem of Mary's conception. The Oxford Franciscan had declared her sinless, the more learned and saintly Bonaventure felt justified only in admiting she was sanctified before birth. And sanctification, as Ware noted, presupposed infection by original sin. John approved of Ware's methodical approach. First, prove the possibility (*potuit*), then the congruity (*decuit*), then the actuality (*fecit*). *Potuit, decuit, ergo fecit* was the correct way to structure his proof. But in view of St. Bonaventure's criticism, he would have to study the saint's reasons for rejecting it.

St. Bonaventure

Living in the Paris friary, where Anglo-Norman friars had come for university studies, Bonaventure knew of this "foreign opinion" as the Italians liked to call it. Unlike his contemporaries, Thomas Aquinas or Albert the Great, this saintly Franciscan doctor had discussed it in great detail in his *Commentary on the Sentences* before reluctantly rejecting it in favor of the opinion that Mary had contracted original sin. This, as he put it, was the more common, the more reasonable, and the safer opinion to hold. It was the more common, since almost every theologian he knew of held it; for Mary had the common aches and pains of humanity that theologians regarded as penalties of original sin; and unlike her son, who had taken these upon himself willingly as our new Adam and redeemer, she would have contracted them, like anyone else not virginally conceived. It was more reasonable, since nature precedes grace, and not just conceptually but in the order of time, for—as Augustine pointed out—one must first be born before one can be reborn, and since the soul is not infused into the body at the moment of conception, but only a month or so later, the infected flesh exists before the grace filled soul can be created and infused into an organized embryo; if its flesh is infected flesh, it is suited by nature to infect the soul, and hence time wise, infection has to precede sanctification. It is the safer or more secure opinion theologically, because it is more in harmony with the piety of faith and the authority of the Fathers of the Church, who, when they speak of this matter at all, say that all sinned in Adam, and no [teacher of theology] "that I have heard with my own ears"—as Bonaventure words it—claims Mary was immune. It also accords more with faith, he insists. For though the faithful have great reverence for and devotion to his mother, it is her son to whom all glory and honor belongs. And therefore it pertains more to the great dignity of Christ that he be the redemeer and savior of all. And it is Christ who opened the door [of heaven] to all, and as Paul told the Corinthians (2 Cor 5:14) since "one died for all, all died." Paul explains this: "He died for all so that those who live might live no longer for themselves , but for him who for their sakes died and was raised up." Hence, Bonaventure concluded:

> And Mary must not be excluded from this, lest by exaggerating the excellence of the mother we diminish the glory of the son; and thus provoke her, who wished to extol and honor her son rather than herself. Let us adhere to this opinion, then, because of the honor due to Jesus Christ, which in no way is prejudicial to the honor of his mother, since the son excels his mother incomparably; let us hold fast to what the common opinion holds, that the sanctification of the Virgin took place after the contraction of original sin.

The problem as Scotus saw it

From his examination of Ware's approach and that of Bonaventure, it became clearer to John what the real problem was and how an effective argument for Mary's Immaculate Conception might be constructed. No one, Scotus saw, wished to question Mary's personal purity or lessen the fact that she above all others should have had earned the highest grace and having committed no willful sin, was as sinless as any purely human being could be. Consequently, the easiest point to prove in any *potuit, decuit, ergo fecit* type of proof, such as Ware had used, was the *decuit*—the fittingness or suitability. All the more readily if she was "beautified with a purity than which a greater cannot be conceived, except for God's."

Fittingness was not the problem. No, the real crux was how to prove that Mary could have been both redeemed and yet not have contracted original sin. This William of Ware had failed to do. It was the *potuit* in his argument that was the weak link. He had not even faced up honestly to the way the common opinion was defended by such great names as Aquinas or Bonaventure. The only alternative William had presented to his own position was Henry of Ghent's peculiar interpretation of the maculist position which he correctly observed could easily be refuted as self-contradictory.

The real difficulty, then, as Scotus saw it was to construct a theologically respectable proof for the pious belief in Mary's Immaculate Conception that would safeguard the universality of Christ's redemption that both Scripture and Tradition emphasized so forcefully. How many hours John must have spent wrestling with this problem during his years of study. How many prayers must he have sent heavenwards for enlightenment. It would be interesting to know just how and when he providentially discovered the brilliant solution he would propose as his *potuit*.

Augustinian legacy of original sin

We can only guess how it happened, but it may have come from studying the weaknesses in the approaches both of Ware and Bonaventure. What was wrong with William's proof of possibility, the *potuit* of his argument? And what was wrong with Bonaventure's disproof? Suddenly it must have hit Scotus. It was their notion of original sin and how it was transmitted that was the stumbling block. Bonaventure claimed that if her "flesh was infected, by reason of this infection the soul would have contracted sin." Ware tried to prove Mary's flesh could have been purified before her soul was created and had touched it. Both arguments stemmed from the legacy St. Augustine (d. 430) had left to the Scholastics as to what original sin consisted in and how it was transmitted. He had identified it with concupiscence, the insubordination of the flesh towards reason, with the unavoidable propensity to all kinds of evil.

This theory, which prevailed more or less unquestioned for some six centuries, was frankly inadequate and created more difficulties than it solved. Theologians, paying lip service at least to Augustine, strove, often at the cost of great subtlety, to free theological thought from servitude to this pessimistic conception of our human condition. This was especially true of the latter half of the thirteenth century when Aristotle's more naturalistic conception of man as a rational animal began to modify or replace Christian theologians' theories as to how much Adam's sin was responsible for our strong biological desires in our pilgrim state on earth.

Anselm's definition of original sin

Already around the turn of the eleventh to the twelfth century, St. Anselm of Canterbury (d. 1109) had produced a totally new definition of original sin as "the privation of original justice." Original justice was *rightness of will* with which our first parents were endowed at the moment of their creation. Anselm calls it "original" because it pertains to the original constitution of human nature as God planned and created it.

It was God's express wish that this justice should adorn the soul of each of Adam and Eve's descendants, but Adam through his disobedience lost original justice not only for himself, but also for his descendants. Hence, we are born into a state that does not correspond to God's will as to how our nature was meant to originate. We should have been born into a state of original justice, but are in fact begotten without such justice. This absence of a justice which is due, that is, which should be there but is not, constitutes the essence of original sin itself. It is not a personal sin of the individual possessing it, Anselm explained, but the sinful state in which the offspring of Adam and Eve exist at the moment of their origin and, one might add, by reason of their origin. Concupiscence, or the inordinate inclination towards sensual pleasure, and the unbridled tendency to satisfy our biological urges, is only a consequence of this privation of original justice. Like the loss of immortality, concupiscence is a mere effect of the sin, one that remains behind as a penalty even after the sin itself is remitted. It is not in any way a part of that sin's essential nature.

Though a far healthier conception of our human condition here on earth, this theory of Anselm went unnoticed for almost a hundred years. It was not until after the great strike at the University of Paris from 1229-31 and the consequent reorganization of studies that it came to be taken seriously especially by Alexander of Hales who introduced it to the Paris Franciscans. But so strong was the old Augustinian teaching, that the Franciscans' master tried to reconcile the new Anselmian concept with that of Augustine. While admitting that Anselm's definition, the absence of original justice, describes the formal nature of original sin, they retained concupiscence as its material component. Strictly speaking, concupiscence is a corruption of the flesh, especially of the biological appetites which tend towards sensual pleasure in an uninhibited way if unchecked. Inasmuch as they are in the body and not in the soul or will, they are not sin as such; but when the soul is infused into such a body, it is infected, for in voluntarily satisfying bodily needs, it strengthens these biological inclinations and acquires habits in the soul that incline it away from God as the one immutable good and towards transient, perishable created goods. The formal and more important aspect, the lack of original justice, is removed through baptism, but the material element remains behind, not indeed as sin, but rather as a punishment for sin. Because of the sin's concupiscent component, the legacy of Augustine, various theories arose as to precisely how the sin itself was transmitted from Adam to his progeny, and whether original sin was uniform in all, or whether it varied in intensity, since one's biological appetites obviously do. Because concupiscence is especially manifest in sexual desire, the idea arose that this corruption in the flesh was somehow associated with the seed; and where parthenogenesis or a virginal conception took place, as in the formation of Christ's body, there would be no need to contract original sin.

Scotus' understanding of Anselm

Duns Scotus was eight years old when Bonaventure and Thomas Aquinas died in 1274 and Aristotelian conceptions of human nature and its natural properties were gradually replacing older Augustinian notions. When Scotus came to Oxford a generation later, the relationship between the supernatural and the natural had undergone considerable change. And Anselm's conception of original sin and its transmission had largely replaced, at Oxford at least, the earlier amalgm of Anselmian and Augustinian conceptions of the Paris Franciscans, also to be found in the theory of Henry of Ghent referred to above.

Scotus had made a thorough study of Anselm's classical work, *The Virginal Conception and Original Sin*. When he came to prepare his lectures on the second book of the Sentences, he raises a series of questions in distinctions 29-32 where Lombard treated questions pertaining to original sin and its transmission. John makes it clear that he can accept Anselm's theory without the concessions that Franciscans, like Bonaventure, a quarter of a century earlier had made to the authority of Augustine.

But we must remember that Anselm died in the first decade of the twelfth century, and Scotus was reading him at the end of the thirteenth century from an Aristotelian perspective. John's conception of original sin, though profoundly influenced by Anselmian notions, as was his conception of free will, bears the stamp of his own intellectual background. For he had his own personal notions, especially as to just how far human nature had fallen because of Adam's sin. As a Franciscan with a deep appreciation of the natural goodness of God's creation, he did not think humanity's fall from grace had so "wounded its natural attributes" (*vulneratus in naturalibus*), as to deform human nature. He particularly questioned the existence of the "morbid quality" that Henry of Ghent or William of Ware claimed to exist in seminally conceived flesh. Consequently, when he came to the third distinction of book three, where his first question is: Was the Blessed Virgin conceived in original sin? he discounts this theory completely. In so doing he pinpoints the source of his dissatisfaction with Ware's defense and Bonaventure's rejection of Mary's prerogative. "The argument that her flesh was infected because of semination does not hold good according to Anselm's explanation of original sin." Sin does not exist in the flesh, but in the soul and more specifically in the will. "There is no more fault in the seed," Anselm protested, "than there is in the spittle or the blood should someone malevolently expectorate or malevolently shed one's blood. What is at fault is not the spittle or blood but an evil will." (*De conceptu virginali*, c. 7).

Scotus' conception of original sin

Scotus accepted Anselm's definition that original sin is essentially the privation or lack of original justice. (*Ordinatio* II, dd. 30-31). But just what did this justice consist in? And why was its privation in Adam's offspring, who had nothing to do with its loss, still reputed to each as sin? Scotus reviewed Anselm's reasoning on the subject. Adam and Eve, said Anselm, by reason of their free will had the power to preserve this original state of justice in which human nature was created. If through deliberate sin that state was lost, however, there was no way the will could restore it. Once they ate fruit from the forbidden tree, their immortality would be gone. "The moment you eat from it," God warned them, "you are surely doomed to die" (Gn 2:17). With mortality came the loss of other gifts as well, the infused virtues that gave their will a ready control and mastery over all their carnal appetites. Driven from paradise they were forced to earn their livelihood by the sweat of their brow, and were subject to all the aches and pains of our human condition. Such was the sorry state to which these progenitors of the human race had reduced humanity. For "the whole of human nature was in Adam and Eve," Anselm insisted, "no part of it being outside of them." When they fell, "human nature as a whole was weakened and corrupted." But though doomed to die, they were still obliged "to be fertile and multiply, to fill the earth and subdue it" (Gn 1:28). But God remained displeased with human nature as they had left it, and though it existed in each of their offspring through no personal sin of the child, the nature still required restoration to God's good favor. Redemption was needed before this original state was no longer reputed to the child as sin. Even when this was accomplished, the effects of the sin—mortality and concupiscence—would remain behind as a punishment.

As Scotus read this theory, Adam and Eve in the state of innocence did not possess the fullness of supernatural life that is given by grace or glory. However, they were created in an intermediate state in which they could have avoided death by not eating of the tree of life, and by the special care of the angels and the intervention of divine providence. Furthermore, they had complete mastery of their animality with all its biological needs and drives. This idyllic state Anselm called "natural," Scotus called "supernatural," and later theologians "preternatural." It was called "natural" by the earlier Augustinian theologians, because it was the state in which humanity was created and was required to be transmitted, and if preserved—after a period of probation—be rewarded supernaturally by the beatific vision of God. It was called "supernatural" by Duns Scotus, because it already transcended the natural condition of man as described by Aristotle. As a rational animal, man is naturally mortal and he was given right reason and a will with an affection for justice to control that "warring of flesh against the spirit" that Paul speaks of as the result of Adam's sin. Later theologians called this original state of innocence "preternatural," for it transcended what philosophers and scientists conceive humanity's natural state to be, and yet it was not supernatural in the sense that the state of union with God produced by the beatific vision in the afterlife or sanctifying grace in the present life surpasses anything a created nature demands in the way of natural perfection.

Through baptism a person is restored to God's kingdom through the merits of Christ. Through the sanctifying grace and the infused theological virtues given by this sacrament, the guilt of original sin is remitted, and the neophyte Christian is no longer in disfavor with God. Infused charity or *caritas*, as its name implies, has made the baptized eminently "*carus*" or "dear" to God. Grace or charity is incompatible with the state of original sin, yet it does not restore the preternatural state of original justice. Grace and the privation of original justice are not contrary states like light and darkness (as the absence of light). They belong to essentially different orders; one is a strictly supernatural gift, the other is the loss of a preternatural gift the loss of which is reputed as a sin of origin. The gift of grace remits this sinfulness of origin once and for all, but it does not restore the preternatural gifts. Hence, the effects of original sin and the redeeming grace of Christ can both coexist in the sanctified Christian soul, as Paul indicates in his letter to the Romans (Rom 8:10): "If Christ is in you, the body is indeed dead because of sin, while the spirit lives because of justice."

But if this is so, Scotus asked himself, why could not grace have been given in virtue of Christ's foreseen merits to Mary at the moment her soul was created? Mary, then, would not have contracted original sin, since the privation of original justice reputed as sin would never have tainted her soul, for sanctifying grace would have made her "dear" to God, despite the fact that she was a daughter of Adam and Eve, begotten of Joachim and Ann in a perfectly normal way. In no way would this compromise Christ's dignity as universal mediator, as Aquinas believed it would. Hence, one major objection theologians had to accepting this prerogative of Mary could be removed.

But John recognized that another problem still remained. Would Christ have been a universal redeemer? Would the prevention of original sin in Mary's soul at its creation have been a redemption? Was not Bonaventure right when he claimed that one must first be in sin before one can be redeemed from sin. Nothing personal of course, but one must first be born before one can be reborn. And it was Mary's birth from infected seed, as the Paris theologians put it, that caused her soul to contract original sin. But Anselm had ruled that out—or had he? Why had he titled his treatise on mankind's sin of origin, *The Virginal Conception and Original Sin*? Was it not to show that Christ's human nature did not contract original sin, because he was miraculously conceived of a virgin and had no natural human father. What did a virginal or non-virginal conception have to do with the transmission of this sin of origin? No one claimed Mary was virginally conceived. Did this mean she too sinned in Adam, as St. Paul seemed to say? Much as Anselm lauded Mary's purity, it was still not clear that his treatise on original sin indicated she lacked that sin as well. A puzzle remained for Scotus' subtle mind to solve. He must study Anselm further.

Transmission of sin according to Anselm

What precisely is the cause or the reason why this non-personal sin is transmitted? Why must it be passed on from one generation to another? Was there some genetic connection? At one point, Anselm had toyed with this suggestion. Biologically speaking, some acquired habits that are sinful seem to be passed on— "the sins of recent ancestors," Anselm calls them. When a forgiving God extended a new covenant to Moses, did he not say: "I, the Lord your God, am a jealous God, inflicting punishment for their fathers' wickedness on the children of those who hate me, down to the third and fourth generation; but bestowing mercy down to the thousandth generation on the children of those who love me and keep my commandments" (Exodus 20:5-6). This genetic legacy is a physical one; original sin is a spiritual one. Yet there is a genetic connection of sorts. Precisely what does Anselm claim this to be?

The saint argued that if Adam and Eve had remained sinless and begotten offspring, the embryo or seed they conceived sexually would not have had either justice or injustice. These exist only in the human soul, and "no rational mind," St. Anselm insisted, "accepts the view that an infant has a rational soul from the moment of his conception." What happens, he asks, when human seed miscarries and perishes before attaining a human form? "The human soul in the seed would be condemned, since it would not be reconciled through Christ—a consequence which is utterly absurd." (ibid. c. 7) No, the soul is created and infused into that seed, that flesh, only weeks later when it has become sufficiently organized to receive it.

But note this, observes the saint. That flesh, seminally conceived though not ensouled, is not intrinsically bad. Had Adam and Eve not sinned, they would still have begotten children sexually, Anselm claims, though never with a mindless drive for pleasure. For their wills would have perfect mastery of their carnal appetite when "the two of them become one body." Eve would have been spared the pangs of childbearing, and it would have been pure pleasure to have become "the mother of all the living." Had their seed been so conceived, Anselm believed, it would be without defect and thoroughly pure, for the soul it needed for completion would have been born in the state God intended.

But the humanity their seed contained in germ, Anselm argued, is a humanity wounded by Adam's sin. For the soul on its creation will have no genetic claim or right to justice. Though the seed itself is not sinful, Anselm explains, Scripture does call it such at times. For example, Job (14:4) speaks of being "conceived of unclean seed" (*de immundo conceptum semine*), and David admits: "Indeed, in guilt was I born and in sin my mother conceived me" (Ps 51:7). And rightly so, says Anselm. "In a man's seed there is no sin before there is a rational soul, but that seed can be called contaminated with sin and iniquity because of the future uncleanness when the seed will have developed into a complete human being" (ibid., c. 14). Yet it is not an absolute necessity that every person "born of a woman," even "born under the law" (Gal 4:4) contract original sin, says Anselm.

The role of the virgin birth

And here is where Christ's virginal conception plays a role, he explains. This was not a conception effected by nature, or the will of a man and a woman, but by God. Like Adam's creation from clay, or Eve's formation from the side of Adam, Christ's human nature was fashioned immediately by God himself from the flesh of Mary. All three, as they came fresh from God's creative hands, were created innocent. This would not be so had Mary's child been procreated naturally, for then it would have been a descendent, a child of Adam. Adam in cooperation with Eve had the power not only to pass on his nature to his offspring, but to give it to them either in the state of innocence or state of sin. He had no such power, however, over one formed immediately by God from human flesh, and not by procreation. Original sin does not reside in the flesh any more than any sin does, but in the soul. Now Mary's soul did not exist when Joachim and Ann conceived her flesh. Like John the Baptist, she was sanctified in the womb. That was what her Feast of the Conception was all about. And throughout her life she committed no actual sin. Far from being sinful when the Holy Spirit overshadowed her and she conceived her son, Anselm insists, Mary's soul was "beautified with a purity than which a greater cannot be conceived, except for God's" (ibid., c. 18). There was no reason why God should not have given the soul of a person so conceived the same original justice Adam and Eve had been given. So far as Scotus could see, this was Anselm's basic argument in this work entitled *The Virginal Conception*.

As John Duns reflected on Anselm's conception of how original sin was transmitted genetically, the glimmering of an interesting idea began to take shape in his mind. He must examine more closely the nature of this genetic bond between flesh sexually conceived and original sin. Anselm claimed it was a necessary connection. Was he correct? Scotus asked himself. What reasons did he give for its necessity? John turned back the pages of Anselm's work to reexamine what he wrote in chapter seven. There he read:

The seed contracted from parents is contracted with the necessity for sin at that future time when that seed will be enlivened by a rational soul. The only reasons for this necessity are the following: Human nature is born in infants with the obligation to make satisfaction for the sin of Adam and of recent ancestors; but it cannot at all make this satisfaction, and as long as it does not do so it is sinning. Furthermore, human nature is not able by itself to reacquire the justice which it deserted; and the soul, which is burdened by the corrupted body, is not able even to understand justice, which can be neither kept nor possessed without first being understood.

Redemption through Christ

What had Anselm really proved and what had he not proved? Scotus asked himself. All he seems to have successfully shown, John reflected, is why Christ's body formed by God was unlike embryonic flesh formed by the will of man, and that there was not the same necessity that flesh of this sort be given a soul deprived of grace. Christ's human soul could be and was created in a state of grace. It needed no sanctification. Hence, God could say to this New Adam: "You are my beloved Son. On you my favor rests" (Mk 1:11). But what of Mary whose conception was normal and natural? All this meant, Scotus argued, is that flesh seminally conceived is owed nothing by reason of its parentage. All such persons are debtors to sin—one could admit—by reason of ancestry. But did this mean Mary's soul could not have received sanctifying grace for other reasons?

If it would have been an affair of honor to reward Adam's fidelity by giving his offspring original justice, it could still be an affair of honor to give Mary, whom he foresaw would commit no willful sin, sanctifying grace at the moment of her origin for the sake of her Son. If sanctifying grace is not simply identical with original justice, it far surpasses it in perfection, and is incompatible with a "privation of original justice reputed to its bearer as sin." All God would have had to do was give Mary's soul such grace at the moment it was infused into her body—a body which her parents had conceived naturally. Because her body had been conceived in a normal way, it would have needed redemption on the part of Christ. But because her soul never contracted original sin, Mary would still have been redeemed by Christ's merit in a more sublime way, because she was kept from being sold into the slavery of sin by reason of her parentage. Though that "sin" was not personal, its absence at birth was a debt every child of Adam owed to God that must be redeemed through the merits of Christ.

Scotus now had his answer to the second problem. Christ's redemption could be extended to Mary as well, even if she was immaculately conceived. For as a descendent of David, and through David of Adam, she had need of redemption, a need she would not have had if she had been virginally conceived as was her Son. Indeed her need for redemption would have been even greater than if she had only been sanctified as John the Baptist in Elizabeth's womb. There was no reason why that debt of honor could not be prepaid, as it were, and then her Son would be redeeming her in an even more perfect way than he would have if she first contracted original sin.

Armed with this help from Anselm, Scotus was ready, he felt, to present a thoroughly professional theological defense of Mary's prerogative, first at Oxford, and then even more forcefully at Paris, where opposition to it was greater than in England and Normandy where Mary's feast was often explicitly celebrated in an immaculist way.

Scotus' Defense

John Duns had his first professional opportunity to defend Mary's prerogative in March of 1300 as a thirty-four-year-old Oxford bachelor lecturing on the third book of the *Sentences*, on the third distinction. His first question in distinction three where Lombard treats of original sin would be: "Was the Blessed Virgin conceived in original sin?"

Realizing that the weight of traditional authority was on the side of the common opinion, as the great doctors of the Church like Bonaventure had explained, Scotus chose a courteous polemical approach rather than a didactic one. He elected to confront the arguments for the opposition before establishing his own thesis as Ware had done. But unlike Ware who had ignored the most common and forceful interpretation of the maculist position in favor of Henry's easily refutable view, Scotus began with the strongest version. Whether or not Scotus had a copy of Bonaventure's question before him as he did on other occasions in discussing a question they have in common, it is interesting to note that John's presentation of the common opinion and the arguments that are used to support it might well have been taken directly from Bonaventure. With a fine feeling for its psychological effect, he proves these arguments for the opposition actually prove the very opposite of what they claim to prove. Though the citations from patristic authorities are many, the theological arguments based on reason can be reduced to two: [1] one based on the excellence of the son and [2] the other on what we see in Mary, namely, she was not miraculously conceived of a virgin mother and in addition has all the frailties characteristic of our human condition that theologians claim are penalties of original sin. These two theological reasons must be answered before explaining [3] how the patristic authorities can be reinterpreted. Scotus challenged both of these arguments directly. The first and more serious he would show not only to be invalid, but use it to prove his own position.

1. The first argument and its refutation

The first and strongest argument used by the opposition, John tells us, was

Christ's dignity as universal redeemer and mediator. Theologians claim this could not be reconciled with Mary's exemption from original sin. As he recounts their contention:

> One reason given is the excellence of her Son, who as universal redeemer opened the gate of heaven to all. But if the Blessed Virgin had not contracted original sin, she would not have needed a redeemer. Nor would he have opened the gate to her, because it would not have been closed to her. (*Ordinatio* III, d. 3, q. 1)

Later, when at Paris, where the opposition to Mary's Immaculate Conception was much greater than it was in England and Normandy, he would expand on this argument.

> The Son of God was the universal redeemer. He was, then, the redeemer of everyone besides himself. Therefore, the Blessed Virgin was in sin, since only a person who has been in sin can be redeemed. For otherwise she would not have been redeemed. Ennobling the mother in the way suggested, would imply dishonoring the Son. Furthermore, Christ by his death opened the gate of heaven to all. But if the Blessed Virgin had not contracted sin, the gate would never have been closed to her, and then Christ did not open it to her. But redemption has for its special purpose the taking away of original sin. (*Reportatio Parisiensis* III, d. 3, q. 1)

From what we have said about his study of St. Anselm, it does not surprise us how John formulates his answer to the claim that the Immaculate Conception detracts from the dignity of Christ.

> It was precisely because of the excellence of her Son, as redeemer, reconciliator, and mediator that she did not contract original sin. For a most perfect mediator has a most perfect act of mediation possible with respect to some person for whom he intercedes; therefore, Christ had the most perfect degree of mediation possible in regard to some person with respect to whom he was mediator; but with respect to no person did he have a more excellent degree than as regards Mary; therefore, etc. But this would only be because he merited to preserve her from original sin.

The triple proof for this is based on a comparison, first, to God to whom she is *reconciled*; second, to the evil from which she was *liberated*; third, to the *obligation* incurred by the person reconciled.

Consider the first, the degree of *reconciliation*. Through Christ's redemption sinners are reconciled to God. But if Christ is a perfect redeemer he will have at least one perfect act of reconciliation. And if that be so, surely it will be his mother that is so reconciled. Scotus puts it this way:

> Christ does not placate the Trinity most perfectly for the fault contracted by the children of Adam unless he prevents someone from possessing such a fault—and as a consequence there is a soul of some child of Adam that

does not have such a fault, or at least it is possible that some soul does not have it.

Consider the second, the degree of *evil*. Is not the perfect mediator he who can free one from the most evil? Furthermore, theologians commonly admit that preserving Mary from all actual sin was a more perfect form of mediation on the part of Christ, than restoring Mary Magdalene to grace after she had lost it through sin.

> It seems Christ's reparation and reconciliation concerned original sin even more immediately or directly than it did actual sin, since the need for the incarnation and passion of Christ is commonly ascribed to original sin. . . . Why then should perfect mediation not be from original sin as well?

Consider the third, the extent of the *obligation* incurred. Is Mary only indebted to God for sanctification in the womb, as was John the Baptist or the prophet Jeremiah? Christ, as God-man, could do better than that.

> A person reconciled is not obligated to the mediator in the highest way unless he or she has received from him the highest good that the mediator can give; but this innocence or preservation from the fault that is or should be contracted can be achieved through a mediator; therefore no person is obligated in the highest degree to Christ as mediator unless he or she has been preserved from original sin. . . . Indeed it is a more excellent benefit to preserve one from evil than to permit one to fall into it and then free such. Also it seems that since Christ has merited grace and glory for many souls, and these are debtors to Christ as their mediator, why should no soul be indebted to him for its innocence, and why, since all the angels are innocent, should no human soul in heaven be innocent except the soul of Christ?

2. The second argument and its refutation

The second argument as to why theologians are so ready to believe Mary contracted original sin is that she was born in a perfectly normal way and in addition had all the frailties characteristic of our human condition that theologians claim are penalties of original sin. Once again we hear echoes of Bonaventure's reasoning, as Scotus explains this argument.

> And the second is based on what we see of the Bl. Virgin. For her procreation was typical and commonplace, and hence her body was begotten and formed from infected seed, and thus the same reason for infection was present in her body as in the body of any other begotten in original sin, and since the soul is infected from the infected body, the same basis for infection was there in her soul as in the souls of others propagated in this commonplace way. She also shared the punishments common to human nature, such as thirst, hunger, and the like, which are inflicted upon us because of original sin; and she did not take these upon herself voluntarily [as did Christ], since she was not our redemptrix or our

empress, because then her Son would not have been "the general redeemer of all." Therefore, these were inflicted by God and not unjustly;
hence it was because of sin, and so she was not innocent.

From his long years of university studies which embraced science,
philosophy and theology, Scotus was ready to explode this myth of the
"infected seed." Though we are indeed created in the image and likeness
of the Trinity by reason of our immortal soul and the supernatural destiny
the divine persons had in mind for us as co-lovers of their nature, we must
remember the spirit within us is a soul, the form of an animal body,
fashioned from earthy material as other forms of plant and animal life that
God made on the morn of creation "and saw that it was good." Furthermore (as Scotus interpreted the Scriptures, with insights from Aristotelian
philosophy), from the beginning, before sin existed, we were created, not
as angels, but as rational animals. Did not God bless the pair he made "in
the divine image" and command them "Be fertile and multiply; fill the
earth and subdue it" (Gen 1:27-28)? Through Adam's sin we have lost the
preternatural gifts we might have had as his descendents, but we still
retain our natural state as rational animals. Was that not why the psalmist
could still exalt the dignity and power God had left to man?

> You have made him little less than the angels, and crowned
> him with glory and honor.
> You have given him rule over the works of your hands putting all
> things under his feet:
> All sheep and oxen, yes, and the beasts of the field,
> The birds of the air, the fishes of the sea, and whatever swims
> the paths of the seas.
> O Lord, our Lord, how glorious is your name over all the earth!
> (Ps 8: 6-10)

Was not all this implicit in John's Franciscan view of creation, particularly in the light of what he had written of the predestination and primacy
of Christ? Christ was the Alpha and Omega of creation, and the whole of
material creation was to achieve its destiny—its "return to God"—through
the humanity the Son of God had assumed. Through the merits of Christ
we could be spiritually transformed as Mary was and our sufferings, when
joined with those of her Son, could have a secondary quasi-redemptive
value, like those of which St. Paul spoke when he told the Colossians
(1:24): "In my own flesh I fill up what is lacking in the sufferings of
Christ." "Infected seed" is nothing more than a metaphorical way of
saying that through Adam's sin we are born in a natural rather than in that
preter- or supernatural state where there was no inclination of our animal
nature to question the will of the mind. With some such a faith-vision,
John must have framed this answer to the second theological argument for

the common opinion that Bonaventure and other great theologians had defended.

> Inconclusive also seems the second argument based on what we see in Mary. For the first claim that her flesh was infected because of semination does not hold good according to Anselm's explanation of original sin which I presented in dist. 30 of Bk. II. Or, even if one were to admit that original sin is commonly contracted in this way, inasmuch as this "infection of the flesh" still remains after baptism, it is obviously not the necessary reason why original sin remains in the soul. For this infected flesh still remains once original sin is deleted because of the grace that is given there. Hence, God could delete original sin in the first instance of the Virgin's conception simply by giving grace at that moment, so that the infected flesh would not necessarily cause infection of her soul; but grace would take away any guilt in the soul.

> The other, about the sufferings of Mary does not prove their conclusion. For a mediator could reconcile someone in such a way as to take from him the useless pains and leave him those sufferings that were useful. Original sin was not useful to Mary; the temporal pains were useful, because through them she did merit.

3. The arguments from authority and their refutation

The patristic authorities cited by his theological colleagues are more or less interpretations of St. Paul's contention that "through one man's disobedience all became sinners" (Romans 5: 19). That is to say, they represent the personal way they understood Adam's sin to be transmitted to his offspring.

> The reply to give to all the authorities to the contrary is that every child of Adam begotten in a natural way is a debtor to original justice and lacks it because of Adam's demerit. Therefore every such descendent begotten in a natural way has a basis for contracting original sin. But if someone in the first instant of the creation of the soul were given grace, that person would never be lacking justice at the moment of origin—and nevertheless this is not due to oneself, but only due to the merit of another, if it was because of another's merit that grace was conferred on this person. Therefore, everyone on their own would have original sin unless another prevented it by way of mediation. And in this way the authorities are explained because "all who are the natural progeny of Adam are sinners," i.e., from the manner in which they get their nature from Adam they have no reason to possess the justice they should have had, unless it is given to them in another way. But just as grace could be conferred afterwards, so it could be given at the first instant [the soul was created].

> This same explanation answers the arguments given for the first opinion, because Mary most of all needed Christ as a redeemer; for she would have contracted original sin by reason of her common birthright were she not prevented by the grace of her mediator. And just as others

would have had a need for Christ that through his merits the sin they had already contracted be remitted, so she had an even greater need of a mediator lest she would need to contract it at sometime and to prevent her from contracting it.

At Paris he expands this argument, adding that

Although in Mary there is found sufficient cause for original sin, God nevertheless could hinder this effect from taking place, even as he can prevent fire from consuming combustible material. Consequently, to be a natural child of Adam does not necessarily imply that original sin is found in that person; otherwise a person would retain original sin even after baptism, since he remains a natural child of Adam after baptism. After baptism, then, these two things are found simultaneously in the same person, that he is a natural child of Adam and yet does not have original sin. Now, inasmuch as there is no greater repugnance in the first instant than in any other, it follows, that a person may be cleansed in the first instant as well as in any other, from sin which would be found in him, if nature had been left to itself.

Mary, then, needed redemption more than anyone else. She needed it so much the more so as a greater good was conferred on her. Since perfect innocence is a greater good than remission of sin after a fall, a greater good was conferred upon her by preserving her from original sin than if she had been purified afterwards. Neither was it necessary on that account that Christ should have first suffered, because Abraham was purified from original sin which was in his person, by virtue of the foreseen passion of Christ. Thus could original sin have been prevented in Mary which would otherwise have been in her.

Note that John is not contradicting these authorities, but is reinterpreting them in the light of insights gleaned from the study of St. Anselm— himself a great authority, especially among English theologians. If Anselm is right, then all that Paul is saying is that through Adam's sin all his natural descendents are debtors to original justice. But debts can be prepaid in various ways. Some, like John the Baptist's or Jeremiah's, were paid before they left their mother's womb. But Mary's could have been paid for even earlier, so that the actual contraction of original injustice never occurred. This, Scotus argued, is a distinct possibility.

But even though he was convinced this was the case, John realized how new and revolutionary his preferred view must sound to others. Logically speaking, it was only a theological possibility. Since he could not expect others to share his personal beliefs, he must deal with the other possibility that Mary did contract original sin before he could frame his definitive answer to the factual question: Was the Bl. Virgin actually conceived without original sin?

How determine the factual question?

That there are other logical possibilities, he had to admit. To deny such would have been not only rash and imprudent, but would have been inexcusable, considering the weight of authority behind the common opinion. As a newcomer to the theological arena, no matter how strongly he felt he had made a good, even a powerful case for an immaculist interpretation of the Feast of Mary's Conception, it would have been an unforgivable affront to disregard the intellectual difficulty of older, even saintly, Franciscan confreres. These respected theological colleagues would have a dilemma in abandoning a belief that in Bonaventure's words, was "more common, more reasonable, and more secure," in favor of the novel interpretation he, a young bachelor, was proposing.

It was in this vein that John Duns turned his consideration to this other possibility. If Mary had contracted original sin, as so many of his theological colleagues maintained, and only been sanctified in the womb before birth, like John the Baptist, how long could her soul have been without sanctifying grace? The interval, most theologians agreed, must have been very short. The question Scotus asked himself was: Could it have been reduced to a single instant? He had heard years ago from William of Ware of Henry of Ghent's endeavor to reduce it to a zero-point. The Ghentian's argument, however, was clearly illogical, violating as it did that cardinal canon of rationality, the principle of contradiction. But Henry's well meaning but misguided attempt suggested another logically viable interpretation to Scotus' brilliant mind. Unlike created causes which produce their effects through a process, God—theologians argued—acts in an instant. If such be the case, then though it is a contradiction for something to occur and not occur in the same instant, there is no contradiction to assert that something that did not exist at one instant, did exist at another. Furthermore, if God creates something, there is some moment when it did not exist, followed immediately by another when it does exist and continues to do so for some time. Since God by reason of his omnipotence can do anything that does not involve a contradiction, he could have created Mary's soul and an instant later given her sanctifying grace for the whole of her life.

This then represents another viable possibility, Scotus assures us. Mary could have been for one instant in a state of original sin and in the whole time that followed in a state of grace. "If this is what the Ghentian had in mind," Scotus declares, "then his opinion is a good one." (*Lectura completa*)

Scotus' definitive solution to the question

Here then was another alternative, not as good as his own perhaps, but the best alternative Scotus could suggest for those who could not accept his own belief that God's mother was absolutely sinless. Our young Oxford bachelor could finally give a definitive answer that was both theologically defensible and eminently reasonable to the factual question he had so boldly raised in his first year as a university lecturer: Was the Bl. Virgin conceived without original sin?

> To the question I say that God could have brought it about that [1] she was never in original sin, or [2] she was in sin for only an instant, or [3] she was in sin for some period of time and at the last instant of that time was purged of it.
>
> I declare the first to be possible, because grace is equivalent to original justice so far as divine acceptance goes, so that because of this grace there is no original sin in the soul that possesses it. God could have at the very first instant infused into this soul grace to such a degree as was given to other souls at the time of circumcision or of baptism; therefore in the first instant the soul would not have original sin, just as a baptized person would also not have it afterwards. . . .
>
> Which of these three possibilities is factually the case, God knows, but if the authority of the Church or the authority of Scripture does not contradict such, it seems probable that what is more excellent should be attributed to Mary.

Evaluation

This masterful argument of Duns Scotus, historians admit, was another major turning point in the history of theology, for it solved the greatest objection that the theologians and doctors of the Church like Aquinas and Bonaventure had in admitting even the possibility that Mary might have been conceived immaculate. What John has combined in the short space of a few pages is a new way of looking at Christ's redemption. It is that which the Bull *Ineffabilis Deus* of Pius IX, defining the Immaculate Conception as a dogma, will describe as *sublimiori modo redempta*. For Mary was "redeemed in a more sublime way," Scotus insists, *precisely because she was immaculately conceived*. This is what Scotus' triple proof was intended to prove and did prove in an amazing fashion.

Word of Scotus' stirring defense at Oxford of Mary's prerogative must have spread quickly, especially among his Franciscan confreres and religious superiors. It may have been one of the determining factors of the English province to send him to Paris, when the opportunity came, to be their next candidate for regent master at that prestigious university, despite his youth and the number of older bachelors who, like himself, were awaiting their turn at Oxford to incept as master.

Mary's Architect at the University of Paris

In Paris, where opposition to Mary's prerogative was much stronger than in England and in Normandy, Scotus seems to have had more than one occasion to defend it, first as a bachelor, and perhaps even as a master. The first opportunity, in March of 1303, coincided with the political appointment of Nogaret the king's minister who masterminded the vicious attack on the pope that led to the shut-down of the university. Despite these distracting circumstances, Scotus' defense must have profoundly impressed a great many others besides Gonsalvus of Spain, the Franciscan regent master under whom Scotus was studying. Writing as minister general in November the following year, Gonsalvus indicates that report of Scotus' "excellent knowledge and subtle ability" has already spread everywhere long before he occupied the Franciscans' official chair of theology at Paris as their regent master. The extant manuscripts that contain student reports of his lectures on the Immaculate Conception are too varied to have stemmed from a single address. One in particular, the Valencia Codex, has the distinctive format characteristic of a solemn magisterial determination, followed by a refutation of some twenty-five objections raised in the course of the disputation that Scotus as a master would have had to answer. It suggests that the legend that came to be widely circulated by fifteenth century writers of a great public debate Scotus engaged in at Paris may not be wholly without historical foundation. If he did debate the issue as master, the actual text of the disputation may well have been lost as were other lecture notes (e.g., of his ordinary magisterial disputations and scripture lectures) in the wake of his sudden departure from Paris for Cologne.

Opposition to the Immaculate Conception

If Scotus' Parisian defense of Mary's conception did not have the miraculous effect of immediately silencing all opposition that fifteenth century legends ascribe to it, it certainly planted the seeds that would bear fruit in reversing completely the thinking of the Parisian masters. For before the century was out, the Immaculate Conception had become the common teaching at Paris and elsewhere. The credit for this transformation must be given largely to the many followers Scotus won to his cause through the writings he left behind for his secretarial staff of friars to complete.

It was the main outlines of his argument in their version of Scotus' *Ordinatio* that we presented above in some detail. Even this restrained and prudent departure from the common theological opinion, however, initially provoked a storm of opposition at Paris, including the accusation of heresy. A year after Scotus' death, for example, the secular master John of Pouilly attacked his views in a public quodlibetal disputation. Though John mentions no names, he cites Scotus' own words at length, answering his arguments in detail and challenging his solution. Pouilly concludes that neither Mary, nor God, her Son, needs our lies; and that inasmuch as Scotus' position is against all Scripture, it must be reckoned heretical and that one who has so taught must be dealt with otherwise than by mere argument. One reason the minister general may have had for sending Scotus to Cologne for his own safety shortly before he died, was that John of Pouilly seems to have had the ear of King Philip the Fair who once before had exiled Scotus for his refusal to back the crown's attempt to depose the pope.

Unlike John of Pouilly, however, other masters were more moderate in their opposition and even admitted that Scotus' opinion seemed to be "extremely reasonable." These were more ready to accept his second alternative, however, that Mary's soul did contract original sin but remained in that state only an instant. But as the older generation of masters died off, the younger theologians were more open to Scotus' forceful arguments. These "new theologians" as they were called, not only repeated but expanded Scotus' line of reasoning. Before the middle of the fourteenth century, however, with few exceptions, it was only the Franciscans who defended the doctrine. During the second half of the century the other mendicants like the Carmelites and Augustinians came to join ranks with the Franciscans in promoting the popular devotion among the faithful to the Marian prerogative. Before the century ended, the college of the Sorbonne at the University of Paris required all who aspired to academic degrees to swear to defend the Immaculate Conception.

It was thus that God in his providence used Scotus' lectures and writings as his historical instrument to solve the serious objections the great medieval theologians had to the immaculist interpretation of the Feast of Mary's Conception that the Holy Spirit was promoting through the faith and devotion of the laity. In the centuries that followed, Divine Providence would enlist others to aid in promoting the doctrine and eventually achieve its official recognition and definition by the Holy See as the dogma of faith. But Duns Scotus would always remain a key figure in the historical development of this dogma. In addition to his sobriquet of "Subtle Doctor" that may have taken on its honorific meaning because of John's defense of Mary's prerogative, in the decades that followed Scotus also came to be called the "Marian Doctor" and "The Doctor of the Immaculate Conception." And through the providential guidance of the Holy Spirit the theological solutions "Mary's Architect" proposed some five and a half centuries earlier would find confirmation in Pius IX's dogmatic proclamation of Mary's Immaculate Conception in 1854.

This then is the theological temple Mary's architect constructed. Small wonder Pope Paul VI hailed him as "the principal standard bearer of the

Franciscan school'' pointing out that "St. Francis of Assisi's beautiful ideal of perfection is embedded in his work and inflames it.''

RECAPITULATION

At the outset of this study we expressed our hope to find in Scotus' philosophical theology some insightful guidelines that are of particular value for professed followers of the Poverello—key ideas that can make more meaningful not only their own lives but those of others who— through God's providential grace—are inspired or influenced by their example or behavior. Example has always been a Franciscan way of influencing others. If reform is needed, it must begin with oneself. And we need to examine prayerfully our own life style. Is it marred by that inordinate imbalance between "individualism" and "community" that troubles so many thinking Americans today?

If properly motivated, Americans by and large can be generous people, and as intelligent citizens of a democratic state are more apt to recognize that respect for their own individual rights is contingent on respect for the rights of others and insuring that universal respect must be a community enterprise. Let us review briefly those notions of our gifted guide that could be most helpful to all of us in this regard.

(1) According to Scotus the source of this inordinate preoccupation with personal concerns lies in the tendency of our will to seek the advantageous (*affectio commodi*). If we deliberately let this subordinate propensity become the dominant inclination in our life, and this is what the utilitarian form of individualism aims to do, then we are failing to live up to and follow the will's most noble and godlike inclination, its *affection for justice.*

(2) "Homo sapiens" is not just a biological organism endowed with intelligence, but a *rational* animal. We are supposed to be guided by prudential judgments, evaluating what is truly good for us, moderating our quest for happiness, seeking to self-actualize our potentialities according to the objective value dictates of right reason. And this means considering what both theology and philosophy tell us about what and who we are, and what God has destined us to become. For man has no purely natural end but one revealed by the God who created us.

(3) Why must we respect anyone or anything? What is the ultimate source of any individual's right? If Bl. John is correct, it is our *haecceity* rather than descriptive properties we possess that gives us our true, inalienable value in God's eyes. And where persons are concerned, it is the individual that is most important to God's ordered universe. But haecceity invests every individual of whatever sort with a special dignity. Every thing in God's creation is our brother, our sister, as Francis poetically put

it in his Canticle of the Sun. It gives us respect for all of God's creation, and especially for this precious earth, our beautiful space-ship, the common property of the human race. We must keep it as God "established it, not creating it to be a waste, but designing it to be lived in" (Isaiah 45:18).

(4) The descriptive properties we do possess, however, are largely complementary in character. As Scotus points out, throughout much of his creation God has joined the causes he created essentially to one another. The manner in which male and female can actualize their reproductive capacity only in and through each other is the model he presents of how individuals can actualize much of their potential only in an interrelated fashion. But if "sex" (from the Latin term *secare*, to cut or to divide) is the most widespread division of any biological species, it is not the only, nor from the standpoint of every individual, the most important segmentation found in human nature. For though each descriptive property we have is shared with some other individual, the peculiar set of properties as a whole may be unique. Even identical twins are not one hundred percent alike.

(5) This unique collection of descriptive traits, our "personality," as psychologists define this term, determines the role we are best fitted to play as individuals. And we need to find the place most fitting for the gifts we have been given. Only then will our full potential be utilized and the aim of expressive individualism, insofar as it is a worthy aim, be achieved. Where expressive individualism fails, in its extreme form at least, is in rebelling outright against all institutional restraint rather than first finding out whether there is not a place within the community that exists in which one can both contribute to the development of others as well as to that of oneself. Whatever the distinctive set of talents we possess might be, they can best be utilized and maximally developed only in a harmoniously functioning community.

(6) If it is an error, as *Habits of the Heart* points out, that the vigorous pursuit of one's own good leads automatically to the good of society, like every great error, perhaps this too is a guess at a great truth. And that truth seems to be, if Scotus is correct, that because of our genetic constitution we can only find our own good in and through another. But we need to realize that the good of society is not just the arithmetical sum of the good of each citizen, but that the good of the whole is something greater than the good of its parts. It is an organic entity. It is something new that emerges as a picture does when the parts of a jig-saw puzzle are properly integrated. Just as in the ideal married state husband and wife through mutual love put human nature back together again, and through procreation pass it on to another generation, so too ideally, if each individual were happily integrated socially, it would be putting human

nature back together as God may have planned it to be.

(7) If the Garden of Eden never existed as a historical reality, the scriptural truth of the Genesis story may well be eschatological. For the first time from the eye of the astronaut we see what our space-ship is like and what the human family, its passenger load, needs to do to survive. If we must move "beyond individualism" as Gelpi insists, it may require more than reorienting the mentality of America's citizens in terms of their national interest. It may mean recognizing the role our nation itself must play in the interest of international peace and justice. As Bellah pointed out, in the midst of each individual's doing his or her own thing, what is needed is a vision. Those guiding the welfare of the state must look outward as well as inward in seeking the best interests of their nation. Like our first president, those who frame our laws and guide our nation must recognize, as George Washington did, they are first of all citizens of the world.

(8) But that global vision must be communicated to the people as a whole. For, as Scotus reminds us, all political power comes from the people governed. If the family is the only natural society God has created, it is the model of how sovereign nations themselves need to be integrated in some organic fashion, where multinational groups play a role but multinational "individualism" is controlled. If the human race as a whole is to become an ideal family of nations, the rights of the least of its citizens still need to be protected, for—as Scotus said above—"In those beings which are the highest, it is the individual that is primarily intended by God."

(9) This is because each person is created in the image and likeness of a divinity that is itself primarily a Trinity of Persons. "Let us make man in our image, and after our likeness," we read in Genesis (1:26). What is most distinctive about the divine persons is how they interact with one another. It is what they do or receive and share with one other in their inner life that makes their divinity a unity. Their personal lives are so intertwined as to be inseparable; in theological terms they form one single triune God. Central and difficult as this mystery is to grasp, it does throw light on how and why we were created as we are.

(10) If an infinite God cannot be duplicated without contradiction, and an infinite God is good, and what is good tends to diffuse itself, to be creative, then the perfections of the divine artist will be spread on the canvas of the cosmos. And where human beings are concerned, there will be a mosaic of different personalities. Like colors of the spectrum these must be recombined into a single beam before the full perfection of humanity can be perceived. This variety within the human species, like the assortment of attributes spread out in the cosmos as a whole, is—

Scotus tells us—a consequence of the infinite self-diffusive goodness of our divine creator.

(11) God's ultimate motive in creating, Bl. John says, is the perfect love the divine persons have for the nature they share in common. Perfect love wants that beloved, that so delights themselves, to be loved by others as well—"willing others to love with God" says Scotus, "the very object of God's love." But God has created us as *human* lovers, and as human we need to love in accordance with our nature. As such our love binds us not only to one another but to the material universe as well. God intended also for our sake "things that are more remote—for instance, the sensible world that it serve [us]." We are, Scotus tells us, "the raison d'être of the sensible world" and through our love and appreciation of its beauty and its goodness, as co-lovers of God and with God, we bring back to our intended ultimate end, not only ourselves and other co-lovers but the material cosmos as well.

(12) But if, on the one hand, man or humankind is an essential ingredient of the cosmos as a whole, on the other hand, as philosophers have pointed out, man is also a microcosm of the universe itself. But the paradigm, the exemplar on which the human nature is modelled, Scotus tells us, is Christ in whom the Word, the "Wisdom of the Father," has become personally involved. "Those whom he foreknew he predestined to share the image of his Son, that the Son might be the first-born of many brethren" (Rom. 8:29). And it is through the grace of Christ, that our human nature is lifted once more above its natural state, as Genesis tells us it once was, in man's pristine state of innocence.

(13) But sin exists as factual reality of the actual world, for as a creature with bodily needs, and born into a world where our need to receive is a requirement for our growth, we are initially encouraged to satisfy those needs. Our affection for the advantageous has a legitimate role to play. But as we mature that need diminishes, and our affection for justice must begin to temper more and more the biological inclinations we possess. Otherwise there will be no proper interplay of the two types of human love of which our human will is capable, and what began as a legitimate quest for self-perfection can run amok and skew not only our own proper development, but affect the environment in which we live. When this fault is recognized and is left uncorrected, it becomes a sin. And, as experience makes clear, such sinful situations do exist, be they voluntary or involuntary, and they challenge the community in a moral way to correct them. For the world in which such evils exist is *our* world, and the primary obligation to change it resides in ourselves.

(14) Revelation indicates how this can be done. Because of sin—says Scotus—Christ comes as a redeemer, rather than as a simple mediator. In

his humanity he reveals how sin crucifies the most perfect of men. But in accepting death on the cross, he merited the grace that we might live and carry on the redemption he began. For we too like St. Paul are privileged to share in his redemptive enterprise, "filling up in our flesh, what is lacking in the sufferings of Christ." And we effect that transformation into Christ, when we follow what he came to teach. That is the path one takes, as Scotus did in donning the Franciscan habit, that he might follow as his saintly founder did, "the teaching and the footsteps of our Lord Jesus Christ" (Franciscan Rule of 1221). It is in putting on Christ, in walking in his footsteps, Scotus insists, that we bring ourselves and all creation back to God. Christ in his humanity thus becomes our fundamental sacrament.

Regretfully we must leave to some future work, a discussion of how Scotus' christocentric ideas might be relevant to other theological concerns or how his discussion of why Mary could be conceived without sin might be relevant to current speculation as to how our "sin of origin" is to be understood.

We only note that it is the personal sin of more immediate ancestors, rather than any original punishment God inflicted on our first parents, that can and does leave damaging effects not only on their immediate progeny but on the human race as well. And this is something we can do something about, particularly since we see ourselves as citizens of one world, and view our community obligations in a more comprehensive and global fashion. Whatever be the specific causes responsible for the rampant individualism that prompted our initial concern, they need to be corrected and the trend they have initiated reversed. If what we need to correct it is a vision, perhaps it is that which Scotus holds out to us. For like Francis, he exhorts us: "Consider, O man, how excellent the Lord made you, for he created and formed you to the image of his beloved son according to the body, and to his own likeness according to the spirit." (Admonitions, n. 5)

AFTERWORD

As we cast a backward glance at the end of this work, we regret that there still remain so many unknown facets in the life of its central figure. To be sure, we would like to have been able to look into the particulars of his youth, to have been introduced to his parents, his teachers, his games, his daily routine. It would have been rewarding to have accompanied him enroute to Oxford and a whole new world. To have sat in on his classes, to have watched him in action in his daily give-and-take with his students as he prodded them along the path of learning would most probably have been a lesson in outstanding pedagogy. To have been in the audience during the ordinary disputations but especially in the quodlibetals, his razor-sharp mind slicing inescapably to the truth, would no doubt have let us see one of the world's truly great minds in action.

To have witnessed his proposing arguments in favor of the Immaculate Conception against the backdrop of contrary views, held by some of the most prestigious thinkers of the Middle Ages, would have presented a picture once again of a mind profoundly concentrating on the matter at hand. We wonder what was his human reaction when King Philip of France exiled him. We feel confident that his allegiance to the Holy See grew from his conviction which few storms could shake. We can also think in terms of his sudden move to Cologne where he took up new teaching duties. We can pause to ponder what it must have been like for him to be struggling to put the finishing touches on the temple he had created.

Admittedly, for those eager to learn of this great man there is something of a frustration with the silence that shrouds many of the interesting details of his life; yet there is a tangible remembrance of him which upon scrutiny tends to summarize his greatness. On September 17, 1966, in the public park of the town of Duns in Scotland, a most interested audience, lay and religious, assembled for the unveiling of the statue of the town's most famous son, John Duns. As the covering slipped away, there stood before them a statue which upon viewing reveals more and more of the depth of the Subtle Doctor.

Strikingly significant of the head tilted upward toward the left shoulder are the piercing eyes, eyes which seemingly scan the heavens for the rays of light which the mind within so ardently craves. Broad forehead and elevated left shoulder bathed in sunlight seem to quietly signal a heavenly communication. Right hand and arm, a quill in the hand, extend across the chest to the left shoulder, as if to receive the message which the left arm and hand extend down to the open volume at the waist of the figure. This is the volume of the blueprints for the temple which this architect has so ingeniously constructed. The final line of the inscription on the base of the statue reads : "Hic magni spirat imago viri." (Here breathes the spirit of a great man.)

The figure in bronze does, indeed, speak. As Pope Paul VI reminds us, the words of Scotus pierce the black cloud of atheism which pervades our time with the message he spent a lifetime honing, an argument from natural reason that a supreme being exists.

Scotus' words, uttered by one whose concern with the individual is legendary, likewise address individualists of our time and our country, admiring our concern for the individual while cautioning the observance of necessary boundaries.

It is in this vein, perhaps, that the figure in the park at Duns speaks to fellow followers of St. Francis: "My sisters and brothers, when I came to Oxford, the spirit of our father Francis was very much alive in our community. We loved and tried to put into practice the Gospel of our Lord Jesus Christ as Francis had showed us. My fellow friars became so good at it, both by word and example, that people from every walk of life and from all parts of Great Britain flocked to them. I know, because I was one so attracted and have tried to model my life on their example. My destiny was the classroom where I was exposed in a more formal way to the significance of the Gospel and the Franciscanism based on it. The lessons handed on to me I took to my room and to chapel to let them sink deeply into my being. Later, in the halls of the great universities of the Middle Ages, I had the opportunity to offer my own application of the seraphic vision to those entrusted to my care."

People from all parts of the world have been intrigued with the works and with the example of this humble Scottish Franciscan. It is love of and admiration for the person and for the works of this magnificent architect of the Middle Ages that have presented these pages, confident that an honest look at the temple he constructed will help us to find the vision to sustain us in coping with the problems of our time and place in history.